Underwritten
by

Century 21

Premier Service

228 West Indiana
Spokane, Washington
99205
1-800-481-0021

-Manito Park-

A Reflection of Spokane's Past

Centennial Edition

The Manito duck pond, formerly called Mirror Lake, circa 1920.
(Frank Guilbert photo, MAC L94-24.81)

Other Books by Tony & Suzanne Bamonte:
Spokane's Legendary Davenport Hotel
Spokane and the Inland Northwest: Historical Images
Miss Spokane: Elegant Ambassadors and Their City
History of Newport, Washington
History of Pend Oreille County

Books by Tony Bamonte:
Sheriffs 1911-1989: A History of Murders in the
Wilderness of Washington's Last County
History of Metaline Falls

-Manito Park-
A Reflection of Spokane's Past
Second Edition

Tony Bamonte

Suzanne Schaeffer Bamonte

Tornado Creek Publications

Spokane, Washington 2004

First edition published 1998
Second edition published 2004
Printed in the United States of America
by Walsworth Publishing and Printing Company
Marceline, Missouri 64658

Library of Congress Control Number: 2004090154
ISBN: 0-9740881-1-0

Front cover photo:
Main entrance to Manito Park in 1906.
(Postcard of Libby Studio photo courtesy Bill Stewart)
Back cover photo:
Overlooking the zoo and duck pond at Manito Park, circa 1907.
(Photo courtesy the Balzer family)

Tornado Creek Publication
P.O. Box 8625
Spokane, WA 99203
Phone: (509) 838-7114
Fax: (509) 455-6798

Dedication

To the memory of:
**Francis H. Cook–"Father of Manito Park," Jay P. Graves,
Aubrey L. White, E. Charles Balzer, John W. Duncan, and
Elizabeth Harris Spence, who as a little girl lost her arm to the zoo's polar bear.**

On July 11, 1923, Elizabeth Harris, a nine-year-old girl, was spending a summer afternoon at the Manito Zoo with her nanny. While there, she placed her hand filled with bread into the polar bear enclosure. One of the bears pulled her arm into the enclosure and the other, smelling blood, attacked it. Attendants came running at the sound of the little girl's screams. When they pulled her away from the cage, her right arm remained inside.

Elizabeth loved animals and insisted no harm come to the bears because of this accident. Shortly after this terrible incident, the family moved to Seattle, where Elizabeth eventually graduated with honors from the University of Washington. She later married George "Skip" Spence, who was also a graduate of the University of Washington. George became a career military officer in the United States Air Force, attaining the rank of colonel. George and Elizabeth had one child, Richard Spence, who now resides in Bellevue, Washington.

Richard said his mother's life was full and rewarding, and she enriched the lives of others by her acts of kindness. She was remembered by those who knew her as the little girl who grew to womanhood knowing no handicaps. Elizabeth passed away in 1981. Both Elizabeth and her husband are buried in Arlington National Cemetery. Elizabeth was a good example of children encountering and overcoming great obstacles.

*Elizabeth Harris,
age 6*
(Spence family photo)

*Elizabeth Harris
Spence, age 25*
(Spence family photo)

Acknowledgements

A special word of appreciation is extended to the following individuals who provided input on historical accuracy and/or contributed countless hours proofreading, editing and indexing (in alphabetical order): **Laura Arksey**, retired librarian/archivist, Cheney Cowles Museum (now Northwest Museum of Arts & Culture); **Carol S. Barber**, past president and member, Spokane Park Board; **Nancy Gale Compau**, Spokane Public Library Northwest Room historian; **David and Betsy Coombs, Scott W. Crytser, Neal and Helen Fosseen, Alfred and Mae Schaeffer, George and Margaret Witter, Doris Woodward**.

In addition, we extend our appreciation to the following individuals and organizations who assisted in providing resource materials and other pertinent information (in no particular order): Randy McDonald and Joel Lengyel, Spokane County Title Company; Jeff Creighton and Susan Beamer, Washington State Archives Eastern Region; Marion Severud, Jim Flott and Steve Gustafson, Spokane Parks & Recreation Dept.; David W. Hastings, Washington State Archives; Kerry Wiltzius and Judy Nelson, The Friends of Manito; Karen DeSeve and Randy Smith, Cheney Cowles Museum; Duane Broyles and Nancy Venziano, Fairmount Memorial Association; Anthony Carollo, Pioneer Title Company; Roy Betts and Harry McLean, Spokane City Water Department; Charles Balzer II, Jim Bolser, Robin Briley, Anne Byers, Richard Coombs, Jeri Curts, George French, Michael Harris, Don and Mary Harvey; John Marchi, Mary Olsen, Jean Oton, Veta and Morris Patton, Frank Peltier, Jerome Peltier, Adi Song; Richard Spence.

Photo Credits are noted within the caption of each photograph. Those from Eastern Washington State Historical Society/Northwest Museum of Arts & Culture are designated as *MAC*. We especially appreciate Jerome Peltier's generosity with his collection, and photographers Barbara Murray, Carolyn Starner and BryanTrent for providing color photographs of the park today.

About the Authors

Tony and Suzanne Bamonte have turned their pastime and passion for writing and publishing Northwest history into a vocation. Collectively they have written and published eight books. **Tony** was born in Wallace, Idaho, in 1942 and raised in Metaline Falls, Washington. After serving as a Spokane city police officer for eight years, he was elected and served as Pend Oreille County sheriff from 1978 until 1991. He has a Master's Degree in Organizational Leadership from Gonzaga University and a Bachelor's Degree in Sociology from Whitworth College. He is a Vietnam veteran and has also been a logger, miner, construction worker, and presently is a licensed Washington State Realtor. **Suzanne** was born in Ione, Washington, in 1948 and also grew up in Metaline Falls. She graduated from Central Washington University with a Bachelor's Degree in Accounting, subsequently becoming a Certified Public Accountant. Prior to their marriage in 1994, Suzanne lived in Seattle where she worked in both private and public accounting.

Table of Contents

Preface

This book is a study of Manito Park and a general profile of early Spokane, Washington. Emphasis has been placed on the visual memories of the past, the key events and the people who shaped the park and its surrounding neighborhood. A vast amount of research data was gathered and analyzed. Much of this information concerns the early development of Spokane, creating the stage upon which the history of Manito Park unfolded. From that perspective, the events and political climate in and around the city of Spokane Falls are intertwined with the park's history. Because Manito Park's creation was a collaborative and evolving endeavor, its history has ties to many of Spokane's most interesting people and events. The narrative contains a number of quotations that are significant to the understanding and color of the times. Not only are they entertaining to read, the quotes also present a treasure trove of historical information. A direct quote from an original source provides substantial evidence regarding a date or a specific occurrence, often resolving historical conflicts regarding times, dates and events.

Manito Park evolved primarily as the result of real estate speculation triggered by the arrival of the railroads and the development of the Inland Northwest's vast natural resources. History has shown that real estate around a park has more value to prospective buyers. Manito Park was the jewel that attracted buyers to the new residential development. It was the spark, now a century ago, that ignited the development of what became one of Spokane's most desirable neighborhoods. Manito Park has been constantly evolving and remains an attractive centerpiece of the South Hill neighborhood. Knowledge of its history is likely to make a lasting impression on the reader's perspective of the city's favorite park.

This year (2004) the community is celebrating the centennial anniversary of when the City of Spokane acquired official title to Manito Park. Though the times have changed, and in many respects so has the park, its honored place in the heart and soul of the community remains the same.

The heavens declare the glory of God; and the firmament showeth His handywork.
Psalm 19:1 KJV

Chapter 1

The Land, the City, the Movement South

In 1862 President Lincoln signed into law the largest land grant act in the history of the United States, the Pacific Railway Act. This law conditionally granted public lands for the purpose of connecting the East and West coasts by rail. Union Pacific and Central Pacific, chartered in that year, were the first recipients of the land grant and connected the East Coast to California. The Northern Pacific Railroad was chartered in 1864 to provide the link to the Pacific Northwest. The law provided over 155 million acres of public lands to the railroads for right-of-way and as a means of raising the capital to build and maintain the railroads. The land was granted in alternating square miles, creating a "checkerboard" pattern of ownership. This pattern, which is still visible on many maps today, was intended to ensure that railroad access across the country would increase the value of those sections of land not granted to the railroad. Much of present-day Spokane was included in the grant to the Northern Pacific Railroad.

The passage of this land grant, designed to open the vast western resources to the East, created a major attraction to the Spokane area for early pioneers, such as James N. Glover, considered the "Father of Spokane." In the spring of 1873, Glover set out from Salem, Oregon, for the Inland Northwest. In his autobiography, he stated:

I had received, from a friend who lived in the Palouse country, glowing descriptions of the beauties and possibilities of the Palouse and Spokane regions. Oregon was becoming pretty well filled up by that time, though, and the idea of getting into the newer country struck me forcibly.

Following Glover's arrival in Spokane Falls, his autobiography continues:

I was enchanted – overwhelmed – with the beauty and grandeur of everything I saw. It lay just as nature had made it, with nothing to mar its virgin glory. I was determined that I would possess it ... The general lay of the land, also, had added to my determination ... I knew the status of affairs with the Northern Pacific Railroad. I knew the company had made a preliminary survey through this country, passing near the falls.

The Northern Pacific Railroad had begun rail construction by 1870, but an ensuing period of national financial depression halted construction until 1879. During this time, several local companies established short lines into Spokane Falls, connecting it with other newly-established outlying communities. Some of these companies were later acquired by the Northern Pacific following its arrival in

Looking toward the South Hill from downtown Spokane as it appeared in 1885. *(Photo MAC L86-275.2)*

Spokane on June 30, 1881. The railroads actively promoted settlement of the new regions to which they extended. The town of Spokane Falls and surrounding region were made to sound like the "promised land" in Northern Pacific brochures designed to lure settlers.

During the pioneering stages of cross-country railroad construction, many hazards contributed to a substantial number of industrial deaths. Tragedy struck Spokane at about 5:30 p.m. on September 6, 1890, when over 200 pounds of dynamite accidently discharged, killing 24 workers. The crew working on a rock-cut at the intersection of Sprague and Division for the new Northern Pacific Railroad freight depot was about to end their shift when the tragedy occurred. Most of the deceased are buried in a common plot at the Greenwood Cemetery. In 1996, over 100 years later, Duane Broyles, general manager of Fairmount Memorial Association, located the unmarked graves and had a monument erected in their honor.

During the railroads-building era, placer gold was discovered in the Coeur d'Alene Mining District, primarily around the region of North Idaho where the towns of Eagle City, Prichard and Murray were established. This discovery, along with vast timber resources and agricultural potential, greatly intensified the growing demand for the railroads. Any means of linking Spokane with the Coeur d'Alenes was a welcomed boost to Spokane's economy. In August of 1885, during the early days of the mining boom in the Coeur d'Alenes, the Nelson Martin Stagecoach Line was founded. Martin's newspaper ad gave the destination as "Spokane Falls to the Coeur d'Alene Gold Mines." His line consisted of two four-mule teams "... well covered with bells, hauling in the first through freight ever coming direct from Coeur d'Alene Mission over the new road to Murray."

Wyatt Earp in the Inland Northwest

Although the early discovery of gold was not the only mainstay of the Inland Northwest, it was a catalyst for a major influx of people – including the notorious Wyatt Earp (of Tombstone, Arizona fame). He speculated in several diverse enterprises in the Coeur d'Alene Mining District and, in 1884, became a deputy sheriff of Kootenai County. He was involved in at least two local gunfights at Eagle City, Idaho, in the heart of the gold-rush territory of North Idaho (nothing remains today of the once-booming community). These events were recorded in the April 5, 1884 and June 28, 1884 issues of the *Spokane Falls Review.*

325   Spokane Falls, Washington Territory.

The above photo appeared in the 1888 book, A Guide to the Northern Pacific Railroad and Its Allied Lines. **This book depicted Spokane Falls as the first point of importance reached in Washington Territory. "It has, in some remarkable respects, more claims to consideration than any other place east of the Cascades."**

On the left is a typical late-1880s advertisement for the Northern Pacific Railroad, which helped lure settlers to the Northwest. (Photo and illustration from **A Guide to the Northern Pacific Railroad and Its Allied Lines**)

As the loose placer gold (alluvial deposits) in the Coeur d'Alenes became scarcer, it was discovered that the real wealth – silver, lead and zinc – lay deeper in the ground. Tremendous fortunes were made. Although the disastrous downtown fire on August 4, 1889 and the worldwide Economic Panic of 1893 caused temporary setbacks, Spokane was well on its way to becoming the economic and cultural hub of the Inland Northwest. Around the mid-1890s, the construction of beautiful mansions in Spokane was testimony to the region's mineral wealth.

The earliest residential development in Spokane was in the immediate vicinity of present downtown. As the city grew, residences were replaced by businesses and larger commercial buildings. The residential district began moving to the outskirts, mainly to the west and south. The first significant neighborhood was Browne's Addition, located on a plateau west of town overlooking Hangman Creek.

John J. Browne moved to the little town of Spokane Falls in 1878, when the population was 54. He was Spokane's first attorney, a real estate developer, and businessman. Although the neighborhood retains only Browne's name, the original developers were both Browne and Anthony M. Cannon. To enhance the neighborhood, home to a number of Spokane's wealthy, Browne and Cannon donated 10 acres for Coeur d'Alene Park (Spokane's first park). Browne built a beautiful home east of the present Northwest Museum of Arts and Culture, which he sold to Robert E. Strahorn in 1902. This wealthy railroad tycoon hired the architectural firm of Cutter and Malmgren to design plans and completely remodel the house inside and out.

James N. Glover
*(Photo from **Spokane and the Inland Empire** N.W. Durham, 1912.)*

Although James Glover, who had arrived in 1873, is historically given credit for founding Spokane, a number of early pioneers were already squatting on homesteads throughout the Spokane area. Many would gain title under various homestead acts. William Maxwell, Spokane's first commercial photographer, squatted on his homestead and built a log house in 1872, which is now the oldest existing house of record in Spokane. At the time, this house at 1735 North West Point Road, situated on a 43.75-acre parcel overlooking the Spokane River, was beyond the city limits of the Spokane Falls townsite. Maxwell officially gained title to his homestead in 1885 and subsequently sold it to William Pettet. The house has since been enlarged and remodeled around the original log structure (see page 15), and the amount of acreage reduced.

Of historical note, Mr. Pettet was apparently one of a few survivors of an ill-fated tragedy during the great westward migration of the mid-1800s. In *Spokane and the Inland Empire* (1912), managing editor of *The Spokesman-Review*, Nelson W. Durham wrote of an incident that occurred in November of 1846:

John J.
Browne

The John J. Browne building at the northwest corner of Riverside and Post was one of the first brick buildings constructed in Spokane. Built in 1883, it was used primarily as a real estate office until the Browne National Bank was founded there in March 1889. It was destroyed five months later in Spokane's big fire. (Maxwell photo, MAC L89-121; inset from **Spokane Falls & Its Exposition**, 1890)

When near Truckee lake they were overtaken by a snow storm at which time Mr. Pettet joined a party of six and started for the Sacramento valley, leaving behind their wagons and about sixty people who, refusing to proceed, camped at the lake. Mr. Pettet and his companions reached Sutter's Fort in safety, but those who remained all perished save four and these were insane when they finally secured assistance.

This description and time frame paralleled that of the Donner Party tragedy, but there is inconclusive evidence that Pettet was a member of this group. He is not included on the frequently published Donner party lists, but it was not unusual for people to have joined or departed from a wagon train along the way with no definitive record. In addition, though certainly the most well-known case, the Donner Party was not the only group to have met with such a tragic fate in the struggle to reach the old Oregon Country.

William Pettet was 65 when he moved to Spokane in 1883. He became one of Spokane's most prominent citizens. Anticipating Spokane's rapid growth, Mr. Pettet invested in real estate, amassing considerable wealth as his numerous properties appreciated in value. He was one of the original partners in the formation of Washington Water Power Company.

Another area, called "The Hill," developed simultaneously with Browne's Addition. This was the hillside south of the city below the Manito plateau, roughly between Stevens and Monroe. As people and the wealth from the nearby mines poured into Spokane, mansions began appearing in this area. In 1896, F. Lewis Clark,

co-owner of the C&C Flour Mill in downtown Spokane, built a mansion at 703 West Seventh Avenue. The following year, Daniel C. Corbin and his son, Austin Corbin II, began construction of two colonial style homes on Seventh Avenue. Austin's home at the end of Post Street, the more palatial of the two, cost $33,000. Daniel Corbin's home at the end of Stevens Street originally cost $17,000 (cost figures from the January 6, 1899 *Chronicle*). Other mansions followed as Spokane basked in its "Age of Elegance." By the year 1900, the city of Spokane was bursting with expansion; hundreds of city lots were surveyed, platted and awaited buyers. In 1903, *The Spokesman-Review* boasted, "Spokane has 7 millionaires" (a mere six years later, another report listed 26 millionaires). A new upscale neighborhood was taking shape and expanding in a residential area around what is now Manito Park.

F. Lewis Clark
(Photo courtesy Spokane Public Library Northwest Room)

Daniel C. Corbin
(Photo courtesy Jerome Peltier)

Within the walls of this home is contained the original log house built in 1872 by William Maxwell, who later sold it to William Pettet. It is the oldest house of record in Spokane today and is presently owned by the Powell family. Insets are William and Caroline Pettet. *(House photo courtesy Valerie Powell. Pettet photos from* **Spokane and the Inland Empire** *by N.W. Durham, 1912.)*

Stanley G. Witter, recreation director for the Spokane Parks Department during John Duncan's tenure, was instrumental in securing the Corbin house plus ten acres on Seventh Avenue for the City of Spokane. Mr. and Mrs. George F. Jewett donated the $15,000 for its purchase. During Witter's 25-year tenure with the City, the acquisition of property was one of his priorities. Witter Pool at Mission and Superior was named in his honor.

Railroad magnate Daniel C. Corbin's residence at 507 West Seventh Avenue, completed in 1898, was designed by architect Kirtland K. Cutter, who married Corbin's daughter Mary. Anna L. Corbin, D.C.'s second wife (previously his housekeeper), is seated between two members of her staff. This house, which was acquired by the City in 1945, is on the Spokane Register of Historic Places and is presently the Spokane Parks and Recreation Department's Corbin Art Center. (Photo MAC L94-40.117)

Pen and ink drawing by architect Kirtland K. Cutter of home built on Seventh Avenue in 1889 for Frank Rockwood Moore (inset). *(Photo from Spokane Falls and Its Exposition, 1890; House sketch from MAC)*

F. R. Moore's long list of accomplishments included serving as the first president of both the Washington Water Power Company and Spokane's First National Bank, companies he helped organize. Moore died suddenly in 1895, at age 43, and George Turner, who became a U.S. senator in 1897, and wife Bertha purchased the home. Moore's estate had been described as "one of the handsomest residences and gardens in the Northwest." The Turners invested another 17 years enlarging and refining the elaborate gardens. The City acquired the property in 1945, the house having been demolished in 1940. In recent years, restoration efforts have resulted in the City's first historic heritage garden (the Corbin and Moore-Turner Heritage Gardens), now listed on the local and national historic registers as a cultural landscape.

The F. Lewis and Winifred Clark home at 703 West Seventh was designed by K. K. Cutter in 1896. The B. L. Gordon family purchased it a little over a decade later, after the Clarks built their beautiful "Honeysuckle Lodge" on Hayden Lake. In 1929 Gordons donated Undercliff House, as they called it, to the Catholic Diocese of Spokane. It marked the beginning of Marycliff High School, a Catholic girls' school. It is now a privately owned office building. *(Photo MAC L84-487-4)*

The fate of F. Lewis Clark, who made his fortune in milling, mining, real estate and banking, remains one of the Inland Northwest's unsolved mysteries. The Clarks had spent Christmas 1913 in Santa Barbara, California. On January 16, 1914, Lewis escorted Winifred to the train station for her return trip home. He then dismissed his chauffeur, walked out into the night and was never seen or heard from again. Winifred held onto the home at Hayden Lake as long as she could, but in 1922, lost her beloved home. She died in 1940, never knowing what had become of her husband.

Looking south toward the Manito plateau in 1891. Today, Cliff Drive, lined with beautiful homes, follows this rim. The large home in the center, at Seventh Avenue and Howard Street, was built for F. Rockwood Moore, first president of Washington Water Power. U.S. Senator George Turner owned it from 1896 until his death in 1932. (MAC photo L86-1035)

Chapter 2

Francis H. Cook, the Father of Manito Park

In his book *News for an Empire*, Ralph Dyar described the arrival of Francis Cook in the following way, "Seventy-four years after the discovery of the Inland Empire, its trading-center-to-be got a newspaper by the grace of God and a tramp printer ... The itinerant printer was Francis H. Cook, a native of Ohio, who had set type on newspapers in many other states."

This "tramp printer" would become one of Spokane's most notable, but unsung, historical figures. He was a former elected member of the Territorial Legislative Council, and although the youngest member of both houses, he was chosen as the president. This was the legislative body that created Spokane County in October 1879.

According to published accounts about Cook, he was a colorful, hard working and honest man. His enthusiasm and faith in early Spokane was the driving force behind his many worthy enterprises. Although none brought him lasting monetary gain, he gave Spokane some of its most notable legacies. He was truly a visionary whose ideas and actions were ahead of their time.

Francis Cook
(Photo courtesy Jan Edmonds)

Francis Cook was born in 1851 in Marietta, Ohio, where he learned the printing trade and purchased his first newspaper at the age of 16. With only $15 in his pocket, he set out for the Pacific Northwest when he was 19 years old. Upon his arrival, he was employed by the *Olympia Puget Sound Courier*. He later bought the *Olympia Echo*, which he operated for three years before starting the first newspaper in Tacoma, the *Tacoma Herald*. While in this part of the state, Cook became familiar with the beauty and potential of Eastern Washington.

In 1879 he moved his printing press to Spokane Falls and started *The Spokan Times*, Spokane's first newspaper. Experiencing difficulties along the way, the first issue, dated April 24, 1879, was printed in Colfax. Spokane's first issue was dated May 8, 1879. When Cook arrived in Spokane, there were differing opinions about the spelling of Spokane. Sometimes the final "e" was used, and sometimes it was not. Cook chose the latter as being more phonetically accurate. He believed with the "e" placed on the end people would give the "a" the long sound. As Cook predicted, Spokane is still often pronounced "Spokayne" by outsiders.

Cook's early days in Spokane were somewhat controversial. From 1879 to 1882, as owner and editor of *The Spokan Times,* he appears to have been Spokane's most ardent and vocal supporter, publicly striving to represent the best interest of the community. Cook's newspaper was the first one in Spokane to receive national telegraph wires from the Associated Press, and the county commissioners declared it Spokane County's official newspaper. However, his opinions often provoked some of the early Spokane community leaders. During his final year with *The Times,* he expressed opinions negative to the character and actions of some of these leaders, arousing their ire. An article appearing on October 25, 1881 stated:

The interest of the ring [Cook's reference to a group of city leaders, namely J. N. Glover, A. M. Cannon, and J. J. Browne] are not identical with those of our citizens. J. N. Glover & Co. must rule the property for which they have already received a price, or do their best to ruin the prospects of the real owners. They are a blight upon the place, standing between our city and the prosperity to which it is entitled. They foster no experience but such as pays them tribute.

This article appears to have escalated an ongoing feud between Cook and "the ring." In response to earlier published statements in *The Spokan Times,* Glover, Cannon and Browne had started a second newspaper in Spokane Falls, *The Chronicle,* on June 29, 1881. A running feud was carried on between the two newspapers.

On the last day of March 1882, this "newspaper war" erupted into violence. Anthony Cannon and his son-in-law, B. H. Bennett, stormed into Cook's office to confront Cook about an article he had written, which Cannon felt was uncomplimentary. Both Cannon and Bennett were armed with pistols. Their purpose was to influence Cook to print a retraction. A confrontation followed that left both Cannon and Bennett severely beaten. Cook remained unscathed, although the stove in his office received a bullet hole in its chimney.

Following this incident, Cannon and Bennett were ordered to appear before a grand jury on charges of attempt to commit murder. By all accounts, there seemed to be sufficient probable cause to support the charge, including motive, witnesses and evidence. However, the grand jury, whose foreman was James Glover, ruled that Cannon and Bennett did not intend to assault Cook and dismissed the charges.

Although many of his accomplishments are absent from early Spokane historical accounts, substantial evidence remains to support Cook's good character. As history plays itself out, the truth can usually be gleaned and analyzed correctly. For example, in James Glover's *History of Spokane* (although this account, which was first published in a series of articles in the *Spokane Daily Chronicle* in 1917, is fairly factual, some of his recollections are not entirely accurate), Glover states: "Along about the same time Francis H. Cook started the town's first paper, the 'Spokan Times.' I gave him one of the finest lots in town in consideration of locating here. It was 60 feet wide and extended clear through from Riverside to Sprague on the east side of Howard street." In later public correspondence, Cook corrects Glover's statement explaining he bought this lot for the going price, saying, "Mr. Glover must have just forgot." The Spokane County Courthouse has a warranty deed recorded on May 4, 1878. The deed states that $50 (the going rate at the time) was received by J. N. Glover from F. H. Cook for the purchase of the property in question.

Above: Francis and Laura Cook with six of their eleven children in 1890, from left, Clara, Frank, Katie, baby Chester, Laura May and Silas (seated).
(Photo courtesy of Adi Song, great-granddaughter of Francis and Laura Cook)

Right: News clipping of Francis Cook, center as president, and Washington's territorial legislative body that was responsible for the creation of Spokane County in 1879.

Upper House of Legislature Which Created Spokane County

These are the members and the employes of the council or senate of the Washington territorial legislature of 1879, which created Spokane county, separating it from Stevens county. Francis H. Cook, publisher of the first newspaper in Spokane, was a member of the council from Pierce, Mason and Chehalis counties. At that time he was publishing newspapers in both New Tacoma and Spokane Falls and claimed residence on the Sound. Mr. Cook, who is president of the council, is seen in the center of the picture. The four men on the left and the four on the right, with Mr. Cook, constituted the council, the others are the employes. The members of the council are (reading down left-hand row), James B. Ballu of the lower Columbia counties, G. S. Dudley of the lower Sound, G. Mc 'Ringer of W----an, R. O. Dunbar of Goldendale, later supreme court justice; (reading up right-hand row) Elliott Cline of W----alin, Dr. J. H. Day of Dayton and Amos Tullis of Chehalis.

Police Chief Joel Warren (center, back row) and the Spokane Police Department, circa 1887. *(Photo from the William H. Lewis Collection, courtesy Spokane Police Department history book committee)*

According to Lewis family records, William Horatio Lewis (above photo, seated second from left) was one of the originators and designers of the Washington State flag. He was an inspector for the Spokane Police Department, having started with the department in 1887. Lewis was the first Spokane policeman to wear a uniform, which he acquired while working as a police officer in Montana. He set up the Bertillon fingerprint system and organized the Police Beneficial. He was among the first white men to reach the Custer battlefield, where he picked up a flute made from a rifle barrel.

By May 1882, both newspapers had changed hands and Cook began his next major endeavor – the purchase of land on the Manito plateau. In May of 1884, he purchased 40 acres from the U. S. Government General Land Office. This sale was authorized by an 1820 Act of Congress allowing provisions for the sale of public lands. The property became Cook's First and Second Additions and took in the area now occupied by the Cathedral of St. John the Evangelist. By the mid-1880s, Cook had established a farm on his property on the hill south of town. For the next few years this would be the main focus of his attention. The *1887 Polk Directory* lists him as a farmer living at "Spokane Heights." True to Cook's style, he met this new enterprise headlong; everything was going to be first class. Several articles appearing in the July 14, 1883 edition of the *Spokane Falls Review* gave a rare glimpse of Cook's farming operation:

Francis H. Cook received this week direct from New York City, a colony of Italian bees, the first of the kind ever imported into this country. The little fellows came through by express order, and already have commenced operations. Mr. Cook takes great pride in securing for his place the best of everything, and at some future day he will possess the model farm of the northeast.

...F. H. Cook, living only a short distance south of this city, has growing on his place nineteen varieties of potatoes, the seed of which was procured from the East, and they are all doing splendidly.

Two years later, Cook made one of the most significant real estate purchases in the history of Spokane's South Hill. On February 4, 1886, he purchased 160 acres from the Pend Oreille Land Division of the Northern Pacific Railroad Company. This purchase encom-

Francis and Laura Cook's nine-bedroom home, which they built in 1892 and lost in 1897 following the Economic Panic of 1893. The home was located at the site of the present Cathedral of St. John's parish house, the Jewett House. Around 1901 it was converted into Mount View (later Spokane) Sanitarium. (Photo courtesy of Adi Song, Cooks' great-granddaughter)

passed the area surrounding and including the present Manito Park. With this purchase was a "certificate of lake," which Cook later named Mirror Lake. At that time, this body of water included the present Manito duck pond and a channel extending to Grand Boulevard. Much of the Manito plateau was rather barren, dotted by pine and cedar trees. The future park site was an exception. Wild roses grew in profusion. There were numerous bubbling springs throughout the area, and a large grove of trees, mostly alder, between Grand and the lake. From the highest point in present Manito Park, Mt. Spokane was visible to the north. Cook called this area Montrose Park (officially changed to Manito in 1903). His Manito plateau investments eventually grew to over 600 acres, which he planned to develop and sell. Though not officially designated, the Manito plateau became known as "Cook's Hill."

Beginning on September 21, 1886, Francis Cook again made history with another Spokane "first." He organized and hosted Spokane's first annual county fair. This event, representing Spokane and adjoining counties throughout the Washington and Idaho Territories, was held on his farm at the Montrose Park site. It ran for five days and included numerous displays of produce and crafts, along with many various contests of skill. Later accounts refer to a pavilion built by Cook. It is likely this pavilion was built at

the time of the fair to house the displays. The predominant events were various types of horse racing, in which Cook explicitly outlawed the use of spurs or whips. It was typical at events or gatherings such as this to test for the fastest horses and most skillful men. Time has not changed that competitive spirit – only the means.

During this era, Spokane was a horse-and-mule town, as were all cities of the nation. Life was from a walk to a gallop, rather than the arterial-to-freeway speed of today. Travel of any significant distance required a horse to be saddled and bridled, or attached to a cart or wagon. There was also the matter of feeding, boarding and caring for them. In addition, they were messy, leaving a trail of manure behind them. One of life's daily concerns was "not to scare the horses."

In 1880 Spokane's population had only numbered about 350 people. Within 10 years, it reached 20,000. Spokane was becoming a booming city, and transportation – limited to horses – would undergo a major change. As discussed in the next chapter, Francis Cook once again emerged as a leader as Spokane evolved toward motorized public transportation. His next enterprise was to have a major impact on the development of the South Hill and Manito Park.

From Francis Cook's Obituary in The Spokesman-Review, June 30, 1920

In later years Mr. Cook acquired and platted all of what is now Cook's First and Second additions and he also once farmed the entire district now covered by Manito Park. When he was in this location he built the first steam line up Washington street to his tract … While living at this location he built a racetrack on his grounds and held the city's first agricultural fair there…

The 1887 **Spokane Falls Directory** listed the following: **Washington Fair Association (Francis H. Cook pres.), grounds one mile south of city.**

The Holland and Shaw Stables in 1924. Until the mid-1920s, horses were the main mode of transportation, and livery stables were as common as today's car lots. At the time, many liveries were full-service establishments offering horse shoeing, feed supplies, sales and rentals. *(Libby Studio photo, MAC L94-36.312)*

Chapter 3

The Later Years of Francis Cook

In 1887 Cook's farm on the South Hill would undergo a drastic transition, greatly influencing the development of the Manito Park area. In July 1887, a lawyer by the name of T. J. Dooley arrived from Minnesota, where he had been engaged in real estate development. Shortly after his arrival, he became excited by the potential of Spokane Falls, especially about Cook's property and its proximity to the town. Two of the biggest attractions of the plateau were its lofty location with an expansive view and, being outside the city limits, city taxes would not apply.

Dooley acted quickly and on the 19th of November 1887, he and Cook formed a land development partnership. Under the terms of this agreement, Dooley agreed to procure a franchise and funding for construction of a motorized streetcar line from downtown to Cook's property, which Cook would build and operate. Dooley would also plat Cook's land into a subdivision of residential lots, creating the Montrose Park Addition. It was to include streets, alleys, boulevards (namely Grand and Manito) and parks. In exchange

Downtown Spokane in 1887, looking east on Riverside from Post Street. *(Photo courtesy Spokane Public Library)*

for Dooley's efforts, Cook agreed to give him sole control over the sale of these lots, with Dooley receiving up to 20% for each lot sold. This contract was to extend for a period of three years.

On December 20, 1887, the Spokane Falls City Council granted a franchise authorizing construction of the motor line. This franchise was given to Cook and Dooley, along with Horatio Belt and E. A. Routhe, for a period of 30 years. With a $25,000 loan made by the Provident Trust Company, construction began in the spring of 1888. On November 16, 1888, the Spokane & Montrose Motor Railroad, powered by a wood-burning steam engine, began operations as Spokane's first *motor* trolley. (A horse-drawn trolley, owned by H. C. Marshall and A. J. Ross, preceded Cook's line. This passenger trolley, pulled by two horses, made its first trip in April of 1888. It operated on tracks from the intersection of Division Street and Riverside to the west side of Coeur d'Alene Park in Browne's Addition.)

Spokane's first trolley line, founded in 1886 by H. C. Marshall and A. J. Ross, made its first trip in April of 1888. Its function was mainly to promote real estate development in Browne's Addition. Pictured above are driver Bill Shannon, conductor John Simonson and city council members taking their first ride. (Photo courtesy Jerome Peltier)

Spokane & Montrose locomotive and crew, circa 1888, from left, Ed Nelson, fireman; Frank LeDuc, engineer; and Peter Mertz, conductor (also police chief, 1891-1895). Silas Cook is at the far right. The other little boy is unidentified. (MAC photo)

Cook's Spokane & Montrose line initially consisted of a square-shaped engine and two passenger coaches. The route began between Front and Riverside, traveled south on Washington Street to Sixth Avenue, where it turned east to a rock-cut on Bernard Street between Seventh and Eighth. From there it proceeded to a point where the Rockwood gate posts now stand. It then continued west on Sumner

to the site of the present St. John's Cathedral, then south on Grand to Montrose (Manito) Park, where the original line ended at about 19th.

A descriptive account of the early Spokane & Montrose line appeared in a *Spokesman-Review* article dated May 10, 1936. This article contains typical recollections of the early streetcar lines:

It was the hardest working line Spokane ever operated. The engine was operated by an engineer and fireman and the two passenger coaches were in charge of a conductor. Peter Mertz, former chief of police, was its first conductor. In leaving the top of the hill, the tram went down nose first but on the return trip, the two coaches were backed up. During the winter in some of the heavy snows, Mr. Mertz states that it took the crew all day to get the little train down and back in one trip.

The tram had no schedule and ran whenever it could negotiate its trips. It had a loud whistle and its engine sent forth such a flood of sparks that anybody could spot its whereabouts on the line. And many of its passenger carried souvenir holes in their clothing burned by the sparks.

A tale is told of a lady passenger who rode frequently on the train in the "rush" hours of the morning. If a passenger didn't manage to get a seat inside and was obliged to stand on the platform, he or she spent her time fighting off the sparks. This is what happened to the lady. Disembarking at Riverside, she entered a department store and was making a purchase when she smelled smoke and suggested to the clerk that the store must be on fire.

He sniffed and smelled the smoke also and was about to put in a fire alarm when he saw that the smoke was rising from the top of the lady's hat. It was one of the little tram's sparks that had snuggled in the beflowered crown and after smoldering for a time was sending up little fumes of curling smoke.

Cook's original Spokane & Montrose Motor Railroad, circa 1889, on Washington Street, just south of Spokane's first viaduct, which provided passage under the Northern Pacific Railroad tracks. When the line began operations in 1888, the viaduct was not yet completed, so early trips began near this point. (E. E. Bertrand photo, MAC L86-1040)

Mr. Mertz admitted the other day that lots of people were afraid to ride in the tram because its cars ran off the track frequently ... Riding the tram was Sunday's amusement venture in Spokane and according to Mr. Mertz, he used to collect as much as $50 a Sunday. The fare was 10 cents. His salary was $1.00 a day – "And I was glad to get it," Mr. Mertz reminisced. Old-timers recall that it was a dull day that the tram didn't instigate a runaway. The puffing, spouting engine with its rain of sparks was the last thing a horse wanted to see.

In 1892 Cook converted the little wood-burning trolley to electricity purchased from Washington Water Power. It continued to shuttle people to and from his Montrose Park building sites, but there was little profit for Cook. He struggled to sell the building sites and meet his expenses. There were only a few dirt roads and no water service. Consequently, the new Montrose Park area remained mostly undeveloped. Mirror Lake and the pavilion, likely built at the time of Spokane's first fair in 1886, were the main attractions.

With the expectation of a promising future, the Cooks borrowed $40,000 on a three-year promissory note from Northwestern and Pacific Hypotheekbank on July 19, 1892. As collateral for the note, the Cooks offered 460 acres of land, including the area on which most of Manito Park and Manito Boulevard lies today, extending from about 17th to 37th Avenue. No doubt this note helped to finance further residential development and the construction of the Cooks' beautiful home, with its lofty view of the city and Mt. Spokane in the distance. This nine-bedroom home (see pages 23 and 31) was the first residence of this magnitude on the Manito plateau.

Unfortunately, the Cooks could not foresee the economic panic that hit the nation the following year, resulting in the worst depression since the 1870s. On June 27, 1893, silver hit an all-time low of 77 cents per ounce. With the resulting shutdown of many mines throughout the country and a collapse of the stock market, the nation entered into a four-year depression. Many of Spokane's wealthy tycoons lost their fortunes.

Cook suffered the loss of his Spokane & Montrose streetcar company. He also lost the land offered as collateral on the $40,000 note in a sheriff's sale in 1895 (Superior Court case #8425). Most of Cook's dreams for the future development of the Montrose/Manito neighborhood and park were swallowed up with the loss of the land. However, records indicate Cooks made every effort to retain possession of their elegant home by selling much of their property adjacent to the home. Sadly, their efforts failed. In July of 1897, the house was lost to the Provident Trust Company in another sheriff's sale. The Montrose Park Addition's thriving future was not to materialize until almost a decade later. By this time, Cook was well into other endeavors.

Francis Cook was 42 years old when the Panic of 1893 hit. During his lifetime, he was dogged in his efforts to achieve success. Laura Cook later wrote of her husband, "The greater the task, the more it seemed to appeal to Mr. Cook." His accomplishments were a better measure of his successes than his financial struggles would reflect. Although bringing life to the future Manito Park and surrounding area is perhaps his most popular legacy, it would not be Cook's only accomplishment.

Looking southeast towards Francis Cook's mansion on the South Hill, circa 1895. The Cathedral of St. John was later built on the property to the right of the house. Note the Spokane & Montrose tracks in the foreground. The houses below Cook's were replaced by Sumner Avenue. Numerous multifamily residences were built in the area of the tracks. (Photo courtesy Spokane Public Library)

Spokane Trail Club at Cook's (now Wandermere) Lake, circa 1920. *(Magee Collection photo courtesy Spokane Public Library)*

On May 1, 1900, a front page article appeared in the *Spokane Daily Chronicle* describing Cook's latest enterprise. It read as follows:

WILL MAKE A NEW LAKE
Fed by the Cool Springs of the Little Spokane
F. H. COOK'S BIG PLAN
For a New Summer Resort for the People of This City
BOATING, BATHING, FISHING

...Plans are being made for the construction of an artificial lake on the Little Spokane river, which will be three-quarters of a mile long and one-quarter of a mile wide. On the banks of this will be a boat house and bathing houses, while in the lake itself will be hundreds of trout of all sizes.

F. H. Cook, who owns 600 acres of land on the Little Spokane river, a short distance above Dart's mill, is the person who is laying these plans. He will commence work on the lake at the latest next spring, and may start as early as the coming fall. The plan is to build a large, high dam across the river at the lower end of his place, high enough to make the water spread out into a lake about a quarter of a mile wide.

At present Mr. Cook owns one of the finest trout hatcheries in the state of Washington and his seven-acre lake swarms with from 30,000 to 50,000 fish, ranging in length from four to fourteen inches. Mr. Cook at present allows no fishing in his lake, but next year intends to throw it open to the public as a sportsman's ground ... He is also building a new sawmill on his place, the machinery for which is expected to arrive any day this week.

Cook had purchased this land in 1889 from the U. S. Government on a five-year contract. His purchase price for 639 acres was $2,196.14. Today, the area encompassing Cook's original development, including his man-made lake, is now the Wandermere Golf Course.

Francis Cook's last significant venture was the development of Mt. Spokane. In 1909 he sold his farm on the Little Spokane to raise the funds to pursue this cherished dream. He devoted the remainder of his life to the development of Mt. Spokane as a public recreation area, which he envisioned would eventually come under municipal ownership. Although it was never owned by the City of Spokane, it did become a state park. An article in the July 18, 1915 *Spokesman-Review* describes Cook's relationship to the mountain:

Looking west over the construction of the Cathedral of St. John at 12th Avenue and Grand Boulevard in 1927. When Bishop Edward M. Cross, third Episcopal bishop of Spokane, located this site, he immediately knew it was perfect for the new cathedral, saying, "A city's churches should tower above its buildings." (Libby Studio photo, MAC L87-1.33378.27)

The Cathedral of St. John in 1954. It is one of Spokane's most magnificent landmarks. In 1961, primarily through the George F. Jewett family's generosity, the Jewett Parish House was built on the site of the two houses behind the cathedral. The Francis Cook home (pages 23 and 31) previously occupied this site. (Libby Studio photo, MAC L87-1.7699d-54)

He Fell in Love With the Mountain and Now Wants All Spokane for Rivals

As the father of 10 [11] children, owner of a section or so of land on the Little Spokane not far north of town and in the 58th year of his age F. H. Cook took a new sweetheart... Mount Spokane. She was generally known as "Old Baldy" when first wooed by Cook, but he rechristened her Carlton, and later improved that to Spokane, with Governor Hay present to attend to the final baptism. Not only did Mr. Cook take the entire mountain into his affections, but more particularly did he take 160 acres of the summit to himself, to have and to hold as a property as well as sentimental claim. He was able to buy the mountain top as agricultural land [a condition for acquiring some designations of government land at the time involved agricultural purposes] ... and Mr. Cook will ask you to produce anywhere another peak 6000 feet high which bears a summit of similar distinction. He has strawberries in bloom up there now.

Still, he didn't fall in love with Mount Spokane ... in an agricultural sense. That was simply an incidental that gave him a place in the sun on its summit. It helps along what ... he proposes to do in adoration of the mountain, that others may feel something, at least, of what the might and majesty of the mountain has meant to him. That others, he hopes they may be counted in the thousands, may share this, he has spent seven of the few remaining years of his life on the mountain whenever the seasons permitted, weaving a highway from base to summit.

... Mr. Cook passed two preliminary summers in surveying his road up the mountain. The result is a road open to automobiles up to within three miles of the summit at what the builder figures an average five percent grade. He is now working on an extension to his mountain home at the 5000-foot elevation ... Less than a mile climb remains, and Mr. Cook is certain that an automobile highway could be constructed to the top.

In this respect the mountain is remarkable, Mr. Cook declares ... It is clothed in luxuriant soil to the peak. The bald spot visible from Spokane is heavy grass. Had he put stock on it Mr. Cook believes he would have had a ready source of revenue. There is certainly pasture enough for herds all summer. The mountain lover doubtless would deem such use desecration. He wants people there. Nothing less than the best human appreciation is the mountain's due.

The Spokane Trail Club in 1923 at Francis Cook's upper cabin near the summit of Mt. Spokane. During the course of his road construction to the top of the mountain, Cook built two cabins along the route, where he stayed while working on the project.
(Magee Collection photo courtesy Spokane Public Library Northwest Room)

A 1912 ceremony at the summit officially announced the new name "Mt. Spokane." A crowd of dignitaries and citizens attended, including Governor Marion Hay (seated behind driver) and Marguerite Motie, the first "Miss Spokane" (inset). Francis Cook is to the right of the car holding a flag. (Photo MAC L86-341.12; Inset photo courtesy Dorothy Capeloto, Marguerite Motie's daughter)

That is why he is everlastingly grubbing away to build a road through the mountain's thick forest. Although alone now, he announces that he will build the road as surveyed if it takes him 10 years ... He thoroughly believes it offers the finest view, the most satisfactory reception and leaves the finest impression of any mountains of all the mountains of the world.

In August 1912, the name of Cook's beloved mountain was officially changed from Mt. Carlton to Mt. Spokane. Among those present for the event at the summit of the mountain were Governor Marion E. Hay, Mayor W. J. Hindley, Marguerite Motie – the first "Miss Spokane" – and Francis Cook. (Of note, Hay was Washington State's eighth governor and, to date, the only one to ever reside in Spokane. He moved to Spokane in 1909, the year he took office, and lived at 930 East 20th. He died in November 1933, and was buried in the Riverside Memorial Park Mausoleum.)

Cook continued to work on his road to Mt. Spokane. By this time, his residence was a modest home at 614 East Wabash, which he purchased in 1910. Much of his time was spent at his cabin near the summit of Mt. Spokane. Although the opening of Mt. Spokane was the major achievement of his later years, his earlier influence on the development of the Manito Park area was his greatest contribution to the city of Spokane.

On June 29, 1920, at the age of 69, Francis Cook died at his home. The cause of the death was stomach cancer, from which he had suffered for the previous four years of his life. He was laid to rest in the Rose section of Riverside Memorial Park Cemetery. Cooks'

oldest son, Silas Cook, who worked alongside his father from an early age, described his father's final trip to "his" mountain, "Shortly before my father's passing, he desired again to visit his mountain that he might, as he put it, be 'closer to his Maker.' Like the prophets of old, he went to the mountains to pray. But he could not reach the summit. He wandered over to Skyline spring and I left him alone."

Winter scene along the shores of "Cook's" Mirror Lake at Manito Park. *(Photo MAC)*

Chapter 4

From Montrose to Manito:
The Jay P. Graves Era

When the 1893 depression swept the nation, it was devastating to those heavily indebted in real estate or new business investments. For some others, however, it provided an excellent opportunity. Those who had achieved some measure of financial security were in a position to take advantage of others' misfortunes. Jay P. Graves was in this latter category.

Graves's newly-acquired mining fortune would increase from Francis Cook's failed enterprises. Cook's small and insolvent Spokane & Montrose Railroad Company, with its 30-year city franchise, became the nucleus for Graves's new Spokane Traction Company. This franchise, which included a substantial portion of Cook's former land holdings, provided Graves with a secure foothold in the Spokane railway and real estate businesses. His enterprising drive would significantly influence the future of public transportation in the Inland Northwest and be instrumental in materializing Cook's earlier

Jay P. Graves
*(Photo from **Spokane Falls and Its Exposition**, 1890)*

vision of Manito Park. Graves became one of the foremost leaders in the development of the Inland Northwest. An excellent book about Graves, *Shaping Spokane: Jay P. Graves and His Times* by John Fahey, is recommended to those interested in the early economic development of Spokane.

Graves's ancestral line is traced to Captain Thomas Graves, who came to Jamestown, Virginia, (the first permanent English settlement in America) in 1608. Captain Graves made passage on the *William and Mary*, the second ship to make this voyage. The family tree reveals a long line of significant accomplishments on a national level. Following graduation in 1880 from Carthage College in Carthage, Illinois, Jay Graves engaged in the hardware business in Plymouth, Illinois. By 1887 Spokane Falls was gaining a reputation as a city of great opportunity. This information, and the lure of the West, drew Graves to Spokane in late 1887. His initial ventures in Spokane were in real estate investment. Many of Graves's early business dealings were somewhat complicated, being cloaked in various partnerships and names. However, his entrepreneurial interests were broad, centering around mining, railroads and urban development. Graves was particularly fortunate during the Panic. By 1894 many of Spokane's founders and early promoters had suffered financially. Among them were Francis Cook, James Glover and Anthony Cannon. In his book *Shaping Spokane,* John Fahey states:

The panic did not destroy everyone, did not maul uniformly. While hundreds lost fortunes and property, a man with money could select among unique bargains in real estate. For example John A. Finch, miner-turned-real-estate speculator, foreclosed Muzzy's Addition; the Hypotheekbank took Cannon's and Cook's additions, and the Provident Trust, Cook's street railway. Sales of abandoned, foreclosed, and tax-delinquent property in and near Spokane would go on for years ... Thus, distress for many meant opportunity for a few. While jobless men occupied the old city haymarket, intending to march with Coxey, by contrast 73 borrowers repaid the Hypotheekbank. A newspaper estimated that there were 650 homeless persons in Spokane, sleeping in saloons or a tabernacle. On the other hand, contractors built a flour mill and 400 new houses (average cost $1,000) in the city during 1894. The state underwrote an insane asylum at nearby Medical Lake and a normal school at Cheney and Spokane County built a French Renaissance courthouse as relief projects. But when the City of Spokane called on individual citizens and business to be sureties for a new waterworks, 155 pledged from $500 to $40,000. Neither Graves nor Clough [Charles F. Clough was one of Jay Graves's partners in development], incidentally, signed as surety.

By 1901 the depression was over and the economy was booming again. For those, such as Graves, who had anticipated the future, now was the time to take action. On November 21, 1901, the first hint of something greater for Cook's Montrose Park appeared in the paper. The *Spokane Daily Chronicle* published a headline that read "WILL GIVE A FINE PARK ... Companies Owning Large Tracts of Land on the Southern Hill to Present a Big Tract to the City of Spokane ... CITY MAY SECURE EIGHTY ACRES."

World Champion Prizefighter, "Gentleman" Jim Corbett, Comes to Spokane

Although Jay P. Graves was one of Spokane's most successful businessmen, his only brush with public office occurred in 1892, when he ran for the position of Spokane mayor. Graves lost to Daniel M. Drumheller, 1,674 to 1,414. At the time, Drumheller, whose home was at 1321 West Sixth Avenue, was very popular in Spokane. The most sought-after dish on the Davenport Hotel's menu was *Saute of Chicken with Mushrooms a la Drumheller.* Even the celebrated world champion prizefighter, "Gentleman" Jim Corbett, had to take a back seat to Drumheller's victory celebration. Corbett was in town for an exhibition fight at the Auditorium the day Drumheller won the election and was disappointed at the small audience. Corbett later said, "If I ever come to Spokane again, I shall take care not to come on an election day. From everything I had heard of Spokane, I had expected to have one of the biggest audiences on my trip."

By 1903 most of Cook's original properties on "Cook's Hill" had been acquired by a number of land speculators. Several of them, including Jay and his brother Will Graves, formed the Spokane-Washington Improvement Company to develop and promote their new Manito Addition, bounded by 14th Avenue on the north, 33rd on the south, Hatch to the east, and Division to the west. Intent on providing reliable public transportation to the Manito area, Graves had acquired the Spokane & Montrose street railway late in 1902. He immediately began converting it from narrow to standard gauge track and improving the cars.

His next step was to organize the owners of the adjacent properties to offer a large tract of acreage to the city for a park. Along with the Spokane-Washington Improvement Company and Spokane & Montrose Motor Railroad Co., the Washington Water Power Company, Northwestern and Pacific Hypotheekbank, and real estate developer Frank Hogan collectively contributed nearly 95 acres to the city. In exchange for this park acreage, the city agreed to pay the costs to improve the area, specifically to build a road system around the new park and bring in a main waterline. Although legal title was not transferred until the following year, Montrose Park took on new ownership, a new name and a definite sense of direction. A July 31, 1903 article in the *Spokane Daily Chronicle* announced the proposed boundaries for the park.

This article also proclaimed the new name for the park "... Manita [sic] Park, referring to its elevation, which affords a fine view of the city." The developers of the Manito Addition understood "Manito" to be an Indian word for "hilltop," as indicated in a brochure they published to promote their Manito properties. More specifically, it is an Indian word meaning "spirit," "Great Spirit" or "a supernatural force that pervades nature," still a fitting description for the area.

In 1907, during a meeting with the Chamber of Commerce, Corporate Counsel James M. Geraghty made a statement summing up the spirit of donating land for parks. This statement appeared in the January 10th issue of the *Spokane Daily Chronicle,* "Let me tell you that no man has ever given the city a site for anything unless it lay near land that he owned and which he knew would be enhanced in value immensely by the expenditure of the city's money on the donated land. A. B. Campbell, who gave the site for the city library is, I believe, the one exception." This statement appears to sum up the origin of many parks, not only in Spokane, but throughout the nation.

Donating the land for Manito Park was clearly a successful financial move for all parties involved and marked the beginning of the real estate boom in that area. At the turn of the century, the most popular areas to live in Spokane were serviced by streetcars. Many of the rail lines were built by real estate developers to promote the sale of their property. In 1903, the year after purchasing Cook's old line, Graves reorganized it as the Spokane Traction Company. With the combination of the Traction Company and his real estate ventures, Graves would turn Cook's former holdings into an enterprise worth millions. Because of its rail access and the city's promise of new streets, Manito Park was at the hub of this rapidly growing neighborhood.

The first Washington Water Power Interurban Depot, circa 1905, was located on the west side of Post Street at the site where they later built the distribution building. This photo captures a typical scene in the era of transition from horses to motor vehicles. The noise from these vehicles often frightened the horses, causing runaway accidents. (Photo MAC L88-408.481)

Trolleys crossing the Monroe Street Bridge in the early 1900s. By this time, they had become a major component of Spokane's transportation system. *(Photo courtesy Jerome Peltier)*

Rapid expansion of the streetcar lines continued as the city grew. Competition became fierce as Washington Water Power began absorbing some of the smaller lines. Graves's line held its ground, but another competitor soon entered the scene and gradually began taking its toll on all the streetcar operations.

Between 1898 and 1899, Spokane residents saw their first auto-mobiles. According to the February 11, 1926 issue of *The Spokane* *Woman* magazine, the earliest photograph of an auto appearing in Spokane was dated 1898. The open car belonged to F. O. Berg. In 1899 the *Spokane Daily Chronicle* reported the arrival of two gas-powered vehicles. The Tull & Gibbs Company bought a large delivery truck. Roy Boulter, owner of the other vehicle, apparently did not have much luck with his – the few times it was seen, it was being towed by a horse. He soon replaced the gas engine with a steam motor, and later converted it into a steam saw.

President Roosevelt Visits Spokane

Not only was 1903 a milestone for Manito Park, it was the first year a United States president visited Spokane. On May 26, 1903, Theodore Roosevelt and his entourage arrived in Spokane on the O. W. R.& N. Railroad. The president's entourage of 13 carriages toured most of the city for over two hours, covering a distance of about nine miles. A luncheon was held at the home of Senator and Mrs. George Turner. (Until her death in 1939, Mrs. Bertha Turner treasured the punch glass used by President Roosevelt). The trip included a stop at Coeur d'Alene Park, where the president spoke to a group of school children.

During the president's one-day tour, the streets for the entire route were watered. From today's perspective, it may be difficult to appreciate the conditions of the early 1900s – most of the streets were dirt or gravel and often dusty, muddy or frozen ruts.

Spokane's first automobile belonged to F. O. Berg. A businessman from Portland had hired Berg in 1898 to travel to New York and purchase a car for him. Berg chose a Locomobile Steamer. However, when he returned with the car, the businessman was dissatisfied with it and sold it to Berg. This photo of F. O. Berg and his new car was taken on Easter Sunday in 1898.

Berg was a pioneer tent and awning manufacturer in Spokane. It appears the F. O. Berg Company (originally Omo and Berg) started their Spokane business around the time of the Great Fire of 1889. They are still in business today, holding the distinction of being one of Spokane's oldest businesses.

(Photo courtesy Spokane Public Library, Northwest Room)

Berg's recollection of his arrival in Spokane with his new car was quoted in the magazine, as follows, "I started from the old O. W. R.& N. [Oregon-Washington Railway & Navigation] depot on Cataldo Street, and before I got uptown I had succeeded in starting five runaways. They didn't have any arrest laws in those days, but I got plenty of abuse." On May 26, 1902, the absence of automobile traffic laws became an immediate problem. Police Chief William W. Witherspoon issued a citation to one of Spokane's leading citizens for speeding down Riverside Avenue. Witherspoon was on a streetcar at the time and caught up to the offender as he reached his destination. Estimating the auto driver to be going at least 12 to 15 miles per hour, the chief issued him a citation. However, the charge was later dropped because there was no law to support it. Chief Witherspoon was on hand at the next city corporate council meeting to initiate Spokane's first automobile traffic code.

In July 26, 1903, this article appeared in *The Spokesman-Review* summarizing the status of automobiles:

AUTOS ARE POPULAR HERE, SPOKANE LEADS NORTHWEST IN USE OF THE HORSELESS – GASOLINE FAVORITE MOTIVE POWER – MACHINES ARE COSTLY – FAVORED BY PHYSICIANS.

No other town in the northwest can boast of as many automobiles as Spokane. The broad, level avenues of the city, together with the good condition of paving generally, afford an ideal place for the pleasures of automobiling. Two styles of machines are noticeable. They are what are termed the "runabout" and the "touring car." The runabout is the smaller vehicle, generally having but one seat and adapted to two persons. The touring car is readily distinguished by its greater size and weight, and may have two, three or even four seats, and is suited for the accommodation of half a dozen or more passengers. The latter machine is also the more expensive, averaging from $1500 to $3000. The runabout can be purchased for from $700 to $1200. Of the three agencies used as motive power – electricity, steam and gasoline – the latter seems to be most in favor. It is asserted the gasoline engine requires less attention and is the most serviceable ...

Speed Was Among Spokane's Public Safety Problems

Because of the frequency of horrible accidents and even deaths due to runaways and other horse-related incidents, Spokane enacted an "Ordinance Relating to Horses." One of the first recorded accidents occurred on November 15, 1881, when the Western Hotel express wagon, with eight people aboard, failed to negotiate the corner as it came onto Riverside Avenue at Blalocks's corner. William Cannon, father of Anthony Cannon, was one of the passengers injured. The 1892 municipal code cited, among other infractions, that riding a horse faster than six m.p.h. in the city or on a sidewalk was a misdemeanor punishable by stiff fines.

Some of the first automobile owners in Spokane appeared to have had difficulties adjusting to this new means of transportation. New automobile owners not only had to be cautious about scaring the horses, but found it important to pay closer attention while traveling. (Photo courtesy Jerome Peltier)

By 1902 the Spokane City Council realized the need for laws governing automobiles. This became a concern when the chief of police wrote a citation to an auto driver for speeding. There was a six m.p.h. speed limit for horses in the Spokane Municipal Code of 1892, but no speed limit for cars. *(Libby Studio photo taken in 1919, MAC L87-1.16861-19)*

Looking south over downtown from north of the second Monroe Street Bridge, circa 1903. The D.C. Corbin home is barely visible among the sparse settlement on "The Hill." (Photo courtesy Jerome Peltier)

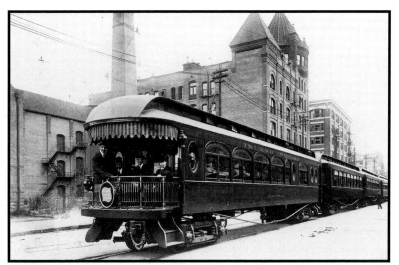

S&IE train near the passenger terminal at Main and Lincoln in downtown Spokane. This popular excursion line carried passengers between Spokane and Coeur d'Alene, with connections to Liberty and Hayden lakes. (Photo MAC L2000-7.35)

Jay P. Graves's early years in Spokane clearly influenced the transition between horses and motor vehicles. The street railway enabled and encouraged the rapid building and expansion of Spokane. The extension of his line through the South Hill neighborhood fed the development of the Manito Park area. Although Graves's most financially significant accomplishment was the development of the Granby Mining, Smelting and Power Company in British Columbia (the largest copper producing mine in Canada at the time), his most important accomplishment in the Inland Northwest was the development of the electric railway system.

The caption in a July 9, 1907 newspaper article read: "SPOKANE TO HOLD A WORLD'S RECORD: Longest Electric System on Earth Owned by One Company." Graves was quoted as saying, "Spokane has more miles of electric railroads than any other city in the Pacific coast states." The article continued, "This statement looks big, but it is substantiated by figures ... Los Angeles comes second with a number of miles less than Spokane." In the final stage of development, Graves's Inland Northwest railway empire consisted of some 250 miles. In 1906, with the rapid expansion of the electric lines, the need to develop a private source of power (heretofore supplied by Washington Water Power) began to materialize. Construction was started on the Nine Mile power plant on the Spokane River (now owned by Avista Utilities). Graves's various rail lines and interests were finally organized into one large company – the Spokane & Inland Empire Railroad Company. In October of 1909, he sold this line to the Great Northern and Northern Pacific railways.

The most tragic railroad accident in the Inland Northwest was the head-on collision of two Spokane & Inland Empire trains at Gibbs, about a mile west of Coeur d'Alene on July 31, 1909. According to Graves's report sometime later, seventeen passengers were killed and between one to two hundred injured. This accident, and the resulting damage claims, plunged the already financially-compromised company into near financial ruin. Soon after, the streetcar lines began to feel the sting of competition from the automobile. In addition, the population count reached a sudden plateau, quelling the need for further rail line expansion.

By 1912 Graves divested himself of controlling interests and responsibilities in both the Spokane & Inland railway and the Granby Mines. His investments in these operations had proved profitable, but many other investors, who delayed liquidating, were not so fortunate. With his proceeds, Graves built a beautiful estate at his farm, purchased years earlier, on a bluff overlooking the Little Spokane River. The estate he named "Waikiki" was designed by architect Kirtland Cutter and landscaped by the Olmsted Brothers firm. (It is now Gonzaga University's Bozarth Conference and Retreat Center.) He also began investing in property north of Spokane, accumulating some 3000 acres, most of which he intended to develop and sell.

The residential acreage market was beginning to soften at this time and Graves needed an incentive to entice buyers. That incentive came in the form of donating land to the floundering Whitworth College, which was looking to relocate from Tacoma to a more strategic site. Graves offered a proposal that gave Whitworth a vested interest in promoting lot sales around the donated land. The college accepted, and a ground-breaking ceremony took place on May 22, 1914. Graves continued to take an active role in the ongoing development of the college and, upon his death on April 27, 1948 at the age of 88, his ashes were scattered at a favorite spot on the Whitworth campus.

Graves experienced financial difficulties in his later years. His real estate investments went flat and further speculation in the mining business was unproductive. He had to sell Waikiki in 1937 at a deflated value. Nevertheless, this shrewd, industrious businessman is remembered for his successes, and seen as a visionary who left for future generations such legacies as Manito Park and Whitworth College.

Jay P. Graves (center in grey overcoat), and other S&IE officers, circa 1910. Frederick A. Blackwell is standing between Jay and Clyde Graves (far right). F. Lewis Clark is second from the left. Fred Grinnell is on the track (center). (MAC 287-70)

Chapter 5

The Development of the Manito Neighborhood

Around the turn of the century, the stage was being set for Spokane's showcase neighborhood. Tremendous wealth from the nearby mining districts was creating one of the strongest economies Spokane has ever seen. Real estate was booming and new housing developments were beginning to envelop the core of Spokane. During 1903 alone, a total of 1500 new structures were built in Spokane. Most of the city lay to the west of Washington Street, with substantial new construction north of the river. A scattering of new houses appeared around the perimeter of the city.

Now Spokane's South Hill was about to emerge with a mighty and lasting force. A real estate article in the June 24, 1903 *Spokesman-Review* stated:

"Top Notch Hill" in the southern part of the town, is quite stable – very few changes in buildings, because people building homes there generally know what they want and can afford to pay for it; whereas the less fortunate ones often keep on enlarging on an originally small house.

This article was defining a developing exclusive area, previously referred to as "The Hill." It also marked the beginning of a name and class reputation the South Hill would retain. John Fahey describes many of this neighborhood's residents in his book *Shaping Spokane: Jay P. Graves and His Times:*

In many ways the Spokane of 1900 mirrored the ostentation of industrial America. As the town flourished, merchants, mining and lumber magnates, bankers, lawyers, doctors and others – even a handful of manufacturers – not only could afford expensive housing, but demanded striking homes to testify to their preeminence in society and business.

"The Hill" was becoming a place of curiosity and awe. People enjoyed viewing the beautiful homes as they passed through this area on the way to Montrose Park (as Manito Park was still called at the time) and the new building lots on the plateau. For an up-and-coming family in the early 1900s, Manito was definitely the neighborhood in which to invest in property for a home. It had all the elements for success, situated directly above one of Spokane's already established elite neighborhoods immediately south of downtown (the area of the D. C. and Austin Corbin, F. Lewis Clark, Kirtland Cutter, F. Rockwood Moore/Senator George Turner homes).

The key to selling real estate in the early 1900s was the availability of street railway service to the development, graded roads and water.

This was the scene of an accident on Grand Avenue between an automobile and the Hillyard-Manito trolley in 1929. Manito Park was one of the most popular destinations in Spokane and trolleys were routed there from every major neighborhood in the city. Note the Cathedral of St. John in the background, which was under construction. (Libby Studio photo, MAC L86-588.206)

When Graves purchased Cook's Spokane & Montrose streetcar line in 1902, he immediately began to enlarge and improve it. He then organized the Spokane-Washington Improvement Company to "plat additions, install water systems, grade streets, establish and maintain parks, and all other necessary functions vital to property development." Graves sold 50 acres south of 33rd Avenue to the Spokane Country Club for a clubhouse and nine-hole golf course. This was a well-executed scheme to attract future buyers to lots around that site. Other developers also began selling lots on the South Hill, and it was soon revealed that a large tract of land would be donated for a park.

Francis Cook's original development project was destined for success – without him. There are conflicts amongst historians regarding the precise point of Manito Park's inception. A number of recorded events suggest a "park of sorts" as early as 1886, when the first fair in Spokane County was sponsored by Francis Cook and held somewhere on his "farm on the hill" (most likely in the vicinity of Mirror Lake). The *Polk Directory* lists "Montrose Park, 2 1/2 miles S. of city on Cook's Electric Line" for the years of 1896-98. In the *1899 Polk Directory*, only the Montrose Park Addition appears and, from 1900 to 1902, both Montrose Park and the Montrose Park Addition are listed. A *Spokane Falls Review* article appearing in April 1888 highlighted Montrose Park as the destination for local picnics and family excursions. Another recorded event corroborating the early Montrose Park was an article appearing in the June 28, 1902 *Spokesman-Review:* "The old pavilion at Montrose park was burned yesterday. The building was not worth

very much. Charles Reeder, agent for the Provident Trust Company, which owned it, expresses the belief that the fire was of incendiary origin." The reference to the pavilion being "old" in 1902 corroborates the supposition it was built during Cook's ownership and development of the area, probably at the time of the fair in 1886.

One of the earliest defining events relating to the development of the Manito plateau occurred on Friday November 16, 1888. The historical narrative of the first motorized trip to the top of the plateau was published in the *Morning Review* the next day. It read, as follows:

THE MOTOR LINE
Public Gratification at its Early Completion.
Comments on the Magnificent Suburban Property.
The Trial Trip Yesterday – A full Description of the Comfortable Jaunt – In Perspective.

"All aboard!" shouted Conductor Peebles yesterday, and as the guests stepped on the car, the engine gave a tug and the long-delayed trial trip on the motor line was fairly under way.

Hopes Realized
For several weeks the streetcar line has been waiting for the Northern Pacific's permission to tunnel under the tracks at the Washington street crossing. At last, however, the owner of the city road, Mr. Cook, decided to operate his line at once as far as it is already completed. He issued a number of invitations for the trip and among those who accepted them were: Mayor [Jacob] Hoover and wife, Councilman Waters, Johnson and Fortheringham

[Fotheringham], J. J. White, city clerk, Chief Warren, City Attorney Houghton, and the representatives of the press.

The Route

The heavy haul of so many passengers up the steep grade along the four blocks on Washington street severely tested the power of the motor; but after a sharp struggle she mounted the hill and turned her face to the East. The engine that drew the first car over the line is a very powerful one of forty horse power with six drive wheels, which are good at holding or propelling. The line runs from there to Stevens street, and after winding in and out for some distance, enters a deep rock cut about 200 feet long. Emerging from this cut the road traverses the side of a high bluff, from which a grand view of the city is obtainable.

Picturesque Scenery

At the Central school [predecessor to Lewis & Clark High School], the eye plainly discerns the far off suburbs of the North Side. From Ross Park to the falls; from the "Hill" to the fairgrounds [now Corbin Park] four miles away, nothing save the foliage of the evergreen pines and cedars, interrupt the view of the thriving and picturesque city of Spokane Falls. The passengers were all charmed with the view and said that no stranger that wanted to see Spokane in its beauty should fail to ride to the end of the motor line.

Ascending another grade we reached the switchback and mounted to the summit of the hill [the site of the present Cathedral of St. John]. From there the road continues on for one mile through Montrose Park and other additions to our city. The land there is level prairie with the best of soil instead of the gravel upon which

Looking north over downtown Spokane from Sixth and Wall, circa 1898. *(Courtesy Spokane Public Library, Northwest Room)*

the city proper is built, and the residences property in that neighborhood will now become quite as attractive as that in any other part of our town. When the end of the line was reached the guests stepped out of the car and were engaged for some time looking at the scenery; and they would have probably kept on gazing until nightfall if the whistle had not warned them to get aboard for the return trip, which was made in very quick time.

Thanks For The Ride

As they stepped off the car at Second street the passengers with one accord thanked Mr. Cook for his courtesy and the ride, and sauntered to their respective homes.

The crew of the train were: Conductor, Cad Peebles, engineer, Frank Goodrich, fireman, John Krick. The regular schedule will be in operation tomorrow. The line will be run with a transfer at the Washington street crossing to one of the company's cars which will be pulled by horses to the Front street end of the road. [The Washington Street viaduct, pictured on page 29, was not completed when the streetcar began operating.]

Although the Panic of 1893 and the depression that followed had temporarily halted further development of Montrose/Manito Park until the early 1900s, with the renewed effort to create a park for the city, the naming of Manito Park was reported on July 31, 1903. The headline in the *Spokane Daily Chronicle* read:

IT IS NAMED MANITA* PARK
Large New Addition on the Southern Hill
BOUNDS CHOSEN

The plat for the big addition which is to be put on the market by the Spokane-Washington Improvement company has been completed.... The addition, which is half a mile wide by a mile and a quarter long, has been named Manita Park, referring to its elevation, which affords a fine view of the city. It is composed

*The spelling used in this article appears to have been a misprint as it did not appear again in discussions about the park.

of 56 blocks of land ... The addition is on the route of the line of the Spokane Traction company, the new street car system being installed by Jay P. Graves. In fact the car line will run through nearly the entire center of the tract. It is bounded on the north by Fourteenth avenue, on the south by Thirty-third avenue, on the east by Hatch street and on the west by Division street. In all it contains 400 acres of land, 320 acres of which is in the city limits. The remaining 80 acres is just south of the city limits .... The two main drives through the addition will be Grand street and the boulevard [refers to Manito Boulevard], running parallel with each other north and south, or lengthwise through the tract. Grand street is being graded 75 feet in width and will have a double car track for the new Graves system. The boulevard will be 175 feet in width, with a 77 foot parking strip in the center, while on either side will be parking strips.

During the spring of 1904, Manito Park was officially deeded to the city by the Spokane-Washington Improvement Company and Spokane & Montrose Motor Railroad Company (Jay Graves's companies), Washington Water Power, the Northwestern and Pacific Hypotheekbank, and Frank Hogan. This gift came with specific conditions, which were outlined in the deeds. They are condensed as follows:

1. The donated park property must be used forever for the sole purpose of a public park.
2. The donation is made subject to the city paying the 1903 taxes.
3. The city shall construct a first-class driveway of not less than 50 feet in width. This drive will service the entire area in the vicinity of the park and is to completed by January 1, 1905. The city is required to forever maintain this roadway.

4. The city shall lay a ten-inch water main to the junction of Division Street and Fourteenth Avenue prior to November 1, 1905. They must forever keep this water main filled with water.
5. The city shall extend an eight-inch feeder line from the ten-inch main to other sections in the Manito Addition. They must forever keep this line filled with water.
6. Since the city will need a water reservoir to fulfill the conditions of providing water for the building sites around the park, the grantors also provide permission for the city to locate, construct and maintain a water reservoir on this newly gifted park property.
7. If the city fails to meet these conditions, the property will revert back to the grantors.

A point of interest regarding these stipulations was the lack of publicity regarding the city's future financial obligation in the acceptance of this land. A number of private interest groups, such as these Manito Park benefactors, had great influence on the local politicians and media, a practice common throughout Spokane involving many of the early parks. Today, this conflict of interest would likely receive much public criticism and challenge. However, at the time, it was key to the development of the parks and their surrounding neighborhoods.

A 50,000-gallon water tower was constructed at 14th and Grand, but it soon became evident that a larger capacity tower was needed. In 1908 the first tower was replaced by a 200,000-gallon tower. This tower was demolished in 2003 to construct a 79-foot tower with a capacity of over a half-million gallons.

The streets were a more challenging matter. In 1907 newspaper headlines read, "GREAT PARK IS IN DANGER, City's Title to Beautiful Tract at Manito Has Not Been Protected – Much Money Spent – Conditions Not Fulfilled" and "CITY DID NOT KEEP PLEDGE – Will Donors Ask Forfeiture of Park?" The reality of what the conditions were costing the city was now apparent. Eventually, waivers were filed in 1911 by the original donors relieving the city of the obligation to build 50-foot-wide streets around the park.

The following year, Jay Graves offered another sizeable donation of land for a park, this time in Spokane's north end. It was also accompanied by a list of conditions. On July 11, 1912, the park board politely declined Graves's offer unless he would remove the contingencies. Four days later, Graves withdrew his offer. In spite of the related costs, Spokane is fortunate to have had individuals with the foresight and means to donate private land for its beautiful parks. Aubrey L. White (discussed further in chapter 6) had a vision of a park within walking distance of every neighborhood and was instrumental in securing the land for many of Spokane's parks. In 1918 a *Spokesman-Review* article boasted that Spokane "leads all other large cities in the United States in park acreage per each thousand population." However, one can conclude that, in many cases, the donations of park land was not purely altruistic acts by the donors who wished to enhance the value of their vast tracts of real estate.

Closely related in both time and geography to the new Manito Park project was the development of Cliff Park (located directly above "The Hill"). An October 17, 1903 *Spokesman-Review* article stated:

Spokane is likely to have one of the finest scenic driveways in the country in the near future. Negotiations are now pending for the vacation of a boulevard site on the edge of the great cliff which overhangs the southern part of the city. The boulevard idea has been formulated in connection with the big park project developed recently for the picturesque area on top of the bluff.

For a half mile the edge of the cliff is nearly level, providing a site upon which a driveway could be graded without great expense. Rugged formations of basaltic rock, the beauty of which can only be appreciated from close at hand, are piled fantastically, forming the precipitous cliff.

Scores of people visit the cliff daily in good weather, owing to the natural beauty of the immediate surroundings and the wonderful view of the city, the valley and the mountains beyond. With a fine driveway all these beauties would be brought within the convenient reach of everyone. The driveway itself would make Spokane famous, as it would be ranked with the most picturesque in the world.

Unite Two Parks

Manito Park and Cliff Park would be united by the proposed boulevard. Manito Park is the 95 acres just donated to the city by the interest which are developing three new additions on top of the cliff and adjacent to the new Graves street railway line. There were 52 acres donated by the Spokane-Washington Improvement company on behalf of Manito Park addition, 36 acres by the Washington Water Power company on behalf of the South Side Cable addition and seven acres by Frank Hogan on behalf of his own tract, contiguous to the other two.

The proposed cliff boulevard would pass through the big new park, and connect with Manito boulevard, the 175 foot driveway which has been laid out through Manito Park addition to the south. The park itself, as well as the resident sections, always will be exceedingly picturesque, owing to the rock formations, the pines and the verdure.

Cliff park is in the center of the old Cliff park addition, the property of the Northwest Improvement company, a subsidiary corporation of the Northern Pacific railway. Cliff park has been platted around a huge rock that is the monarch of all the cliff region, towering from 75 to 100 feet above the uplands. This great rock is nearly an acre in size and except to the most expert is now accessible only at one place. Its precipitous sides in some places have the same fluted formation as the giant's causeway on the coast of Ireland, while in others the crumbling black basalt has been interwoven with vines and covered with clinging moss. The park which has been dedicated to the city consists of about seven acres, including the great rock.

Simultaneous with the development of the Manito and Cliff Park Additions was the growth and expansion of the Cannon Hill neighborhood. This area encompassed the southwest corridor to Cook's hill. It encompassed the region from the freeway south to 29th Avenue, and from Bernard west to the bluff overlooking Hangman Creek. Although commonly known as Cannon Hill, it includes numerous additions, including Cannon's Addition and Cannon Hill Addition. The following is a sample real estate advertisement that appeared in the March 8, 1888 *Spokane Daily Chronicle:*

Arlington Heights of
Cannon's Addition

In the most beautiful location for fine residences in Spokane Falls. It is now for the first time on the market though parties desiring beautiful homesites have been trying to buy lots in it for years. It consists of 25 blocks finely located on an elevation which commands a view of the entire city and a prospect of the mountains and surrounding country which can not be excelled. It is but three-fourths of a mile from the post office. We will take pleasure in showing the property to those who may desire to examine it. The terms will be easy and price low. Sale will begin on Wednesday the 7th, and those who apply first will secure first choice.

Clough and Graves and H. Bolster & Co. Sole Agents

Anthony M. Cannon, the developer of Cannon's Addition, arrived in Spokane in 1878. With his business partner J. J. Browne, they purchased half of the original townsite from James Glover. Among other enterprises, Cannon started Spokane's first bank, the Bank of Spokane Falls, in his mercantile store. In the early 1880s, he acquired 160 acres adjacent to the townsite through a government land grant. A condition for obtaining title to such land was that the grantee reside on the site. Cannon was not adhering to this requirement and almost lost it to a squatter. However, a group of unidentified men influenced the squatter to vacate by firing numerous volleys of gunfire into his cabin. It was later suspected the assailants came from a party Cannon was holding the evening of the attack. Many articles written about Cannon, both in early newspapers and books, portray him as a great achiever and also somewhat of a hothead

(see the Cannon/Cook altercation in chapter 2). Cannon, at one time among Spokane's wealthiest men, amassed most of his fortune from real estate development, especially during the rebuilding of Spokane following the Great Fire of 1889.

About the time of Cannon's arrival, the railroads began connecting Spokane to the outside world. Spokane's population jumped from about 300 in 1880 to over 19,000 in 1890. By 1891 the city limits stretched south to 29th Avenue. (As may be recalled, when Cook bought over 600 acres on the Manito plateau, most of it was outside the city limits, which then extended only to 14th.) The 1915 federal census (as published in the *Polk Directory*) placed the population figure at 139,323. With such rapid expansion, the community faced the problem of where to bury its dead. This was of some consequence to the early land developers. Typically, cemeteries are established during the early stages of settlement. They are usually situated in some of the most prime locations in a community, often becoming coveted building sites as view property and other choice sites become scarce. Such was the fate affecting two of Spokane's first cemeteries, which were in the path of residential expansion. There are many conflicting stories regarding these burial grounds, some of which may be clarified by the following quote from the May 26, 1897 *Spokesman-Review*. It provides excellent descriptions for both these cemeteries:

THE OLD CEMETERY
Movement to Remove One of Spokane's Landmarks
– Pioneers Were Buried In It –
Oldest Settlers Do Not Remember When It Was Started
– Bodies to Be Exhumed

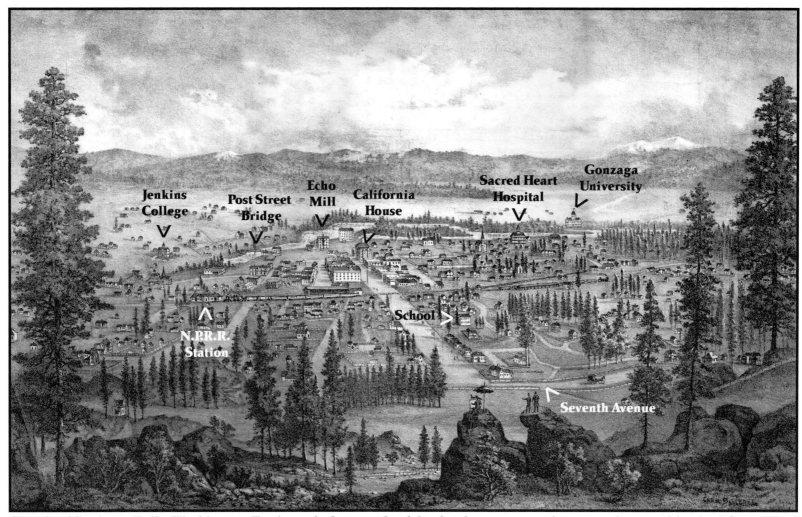

Sketch of Spokane Falls, Washington Territory, before much of the development seen here was destroyed by the "Great Fire" of 1889. (Sketch from Taylor and Jefferson, Real Estate and Investors' Agents, courtesy Spokane Public Library, Northwest Room.)

A movement is on foot to remove one of the most important historical landmarks in Spokane. Last week a petition prepared by J. W. Witherop and signed by W. J. C. Wakefield, John Finch, J. J. Browne, Dr. W. W. Potter and other residents of Browne's addition, was presented to the city council, asking that 17 bodies buried in the old cemetery near the end of the boulevard and Pacific avenue [Browne's Addition] be exhumed and reinterred in one of the modern cemeteries--either Greenwood or Fairmount. The petition stated the matter briefly, pointing out that the west end is rapidly becoming the most beautiful residence portion of the city, that the remains of most of those buried in the cemetery had been removed some time ago, and it would add to the attractiveness of the neighborhood if the remainder were removed.

This was Spokane's first cemetery. Here it was that many of the sturdy pioneers who came over the trail from Oregon, or from the far east, years before the Northern Pacific railroad was dreamed of, were buried, as were their wives, and in many instances their children. How the location was selected as a cemetery no one remembers. It was certainly a sublime spot, however, situated on the abutting point of land, wrapt [sic] in the dense solitude of the primeval forest, commanding one grand, sublime view of rugged cliff and ... the valleys of Hangman creek and the Spokane.

The exact date of the cemetery's first burial is unknown, as were also the burials of later times. No tombstone was ever erected in the plot; only some plain wooden slabs, lettered by the hands of some loving father, husband or brother, told for a few brief months the name of the departed.

In speaking of the old grave yard yesterday, James N. Glover, Spokane's oldest pioneer, said: "Yes, I understand the old cemetery is to be removed. This was Spokane's first cemetery. I do not know just how old it is; It was there when I first came, and used for many years afterward. About 12 years ago most of the remains were removed. I thought all, but it seems not. No, I do not know the names of those buried out there, for I do not know how many or who were removed." J. J. Browne, on whose land the cemetery was located, was more familiar with the later history of the cemetery than Mr. Glover.

"This," said Mr. Browne, "was Spokane's first burying ground. How it came to be selected I do not know; it was already located when I arrived. That was before it came to be surveyed, and was sold as government land. When I got the land from the government the cemetery was included in my purchase, and people continued to use it for many years afterward. That was probably 18 years ago. The cemetery was used until about 12 years ago, when the most of the bodies were exhumed by friends and taken to Spokane's second cemetery, the old burying ground in what is now known as Cannon's Addition, probably a half mile south of the Irving school. This latter cemetery was not used but a few years, the town growing so rapidly that the cemetery was abandoned and the bodies were again exhumed, most of them taken to Greenwood or Fairmount. I believe the number of bodies named in the petition as being still buried in the old cemetery is erroneous. The petition say 17, but I believe there are no more than six or seven. Do I know the names of those buried? No; or at least not many of them. I remember attending a number of the funerals, however, the first funeral I attended in the city was that of Mr. Lowry, a young man, 21 years of age, who worked in one of the mills, if I remember rightly.

First Memorial Day celebration in Spokane. Police Chief Joel Warren, who was elected chief in 1887, and his deputies leading a procession to the old cemetery on Cannon Hill, circa 1887. *(Photo **Spokane and the Inland Empire**, N. W. Durham, 1912)*

... Another funeral I attended was that of Mrs. Evans... She remains buried in the cemetery. Another, and the only remaining case that I know of, is that of a Mr. Evans, who lost his life in a logjam up the river. He was buried there, and only last week his wife came to see me to learn if the remains could not be removed to Greenwood or Fairmount. I thought the proposal impossible, but she felt sure that she could identify the remains if they were exhumed. She said that Mr. Evans lost his life up the river, and that his skull was fractured in such a way that she could never forget it, or fail to identify the remains. The fracture was on the side of the head, and she still remembered how it looked. I also remember the burial of a number of men killed in a wreck on the Northern Pacific trestle, just north of the city, when that road was being built through the city... A number of the Havermale children were also buried there...

Mountain View, another of the first cemeteries, appeared on early maps between Cedar and Ash from about 10th to 12th Avenue (part of the Cannon Hill neighborhood). It began receiving bodies as early as 1881, but was not officially declared a cemetery until the fall of 1883. Anthony Cannon was one of the early residents who had planned on Mountain View as his final resting place. The November 17, 1883 issue of the *Spokane Falls Review* contains a lengthy description of Mountain View Cemetery. An excerpt follows:

About one mile southwest of the center of Spokane Falls is situated "Mountain View Cemetery," the city of our dead. The location has been well chosen, and the name, recently adopted, in every respect appropriate. This necropolis occupies a clear space of some 40 acres, on a ridge overlooking Hangman creek, and is surrounded with a forest of noble pines. The piece of ground was dedicated to the purpose for which it is used last spring, and already is dotted here and there with those slim, rounded mounds that indicate the last resting place of those near and dear to the members of our community... We see that a number of persons have made the right move in this direction, several neat headstones having been put in place during the past week. In this Mr. A. M. Cannon has taken the lead. On his lot near the center of the grounds, he has had a handsome monument erected. It is a square shaft of Italian marble ...The four sides of the shaft are smooth, leaving spaces for future inscriptions ... at base of shaft, is the single name "Clarke," while on the west side, in the same position, is the name "Cannon". Above on the east side, is the inscription, "George P. Clarke [Cannon's stepson], born June 23, 1867, died April 5, 1883." [The monument was later moved to Greenwood Cemetery.] ... It is a quiet place to sleep that sleep of eternity ...

Mountain View Cemetery was officially discontinued in June of 1888, when the city council and the county commissioners selected Fairmount Cemetery, incorporated that year, as Spokane's official burial grounds. On May 12, 1888, Anthony Cannon, along with four partners, developed and incorporated Greenwood Cemetery. The bodies from Mountain View were exhumed and removed to Greenwood and Fairmount. Early politics clearly played a role in this event. Cannon had just completed a two-year term as the mayor of Spokane Falls, had previously served as a city councilman, and was well ingrained with the "city powers." Within five months of leaving office on May 23, 1888, the city council passed an ordinance stating: "No body or remains of any deceased person shall be interred or buried in any cemetery, burial ground or other place within the city limits." Mountain View was within the city limits; Greenwood and Fairmount were not. Cannon held 360 of the 500 Greenwood shares.

Anthony Cannon, circa 1890. *(Photo from Spokane Falls and Its Exposition, 1890)*

Following the removal of Mountain View Cemetery from Cannon Hill, a rich showcase of homes, built in the late 1880s to about 1913, filled in the surrounding neighborhood. During the Depression years of the 1930s, many of the large older homes were converted to apartments. Later, because of lenient zoning regulations, numerous apartment houses were built on many of the remaining lots. A number of social-rehabilitation homes have also been concentrated in this area, typically located in some of the original homes. In the era of

Francis and Anna Motie and family during the construction of their home at 614 West Thirteenth in 1909. The Moties had eight daughters, one of whom, Marquerite, became the first Miss Spokane, the official city hostess, in 1912. (Photo courtesy Dororthy Capeloto, Marquerite's daughter.)

the original single-family homes (classified as Grid #40 on the Spokane real estate maps), this was one of Spokane's most beautiful neighborhoods and was inhabited largely by medical and business professionals. The styles of homes in this neighborhood are eclectic, ranging from Victorian and American Four-Square to Colonial Revival. By the time the Manito Park neighborhood began to develop, the Cannon Hill area was fairly populated. There was a natural geographical corridor between the two areas, making Manito Park a favorite and frequently used recreation area for Cannon Hill residents.

242 E. Manito Place

This house was designed in 1907 by the architectural firm of George Keith and Harold Whitehouse. It was built for Daniel Morgan, vice-president of Fred Grinnell's company. Keith also designed the Royal Riblet mansion (now the Arbor Crest Winery). Whitehouse is best known as the architect who designed St. John's Cathedral on Grand Boulevard.

Between the years of 1922 and 1928, Morgan served one term in the State House of Representatives and two in the State Senate. During his tenure as a public servant, he was instrumental in securing legislation for the development of the Columbia Basin. Morgan died in Spokane at the age of 93. He spent most of his life in the Inland Northwest and, for many years, was a trustee for the Chamber of Commerce.

By 1907 the Manito area entered a steady growth pattern. During that year, Jay P. Graves hired Fred Grinnell, a seasoned real estate salesman, to sell his property. Grinnell owned one of the largest real estate companies in Spokane. His office was located at the intersection of Main and Lincoln Street on the main floor of the Interurban Terminal Building (now the location of the main branch of the Spokane Public Library). Upon assuming responsibility for the sales of the Spokane-Washington

Fred Grinnell
(Photo MAC detail of L95-6.28)

Improvement Company's land for Graves and partners, he set up an office at the southwest corner of 29th and Grand, and later added a smaller office at the intersection of 21st and Grand, across from Manito Park. Grinnell had a reputation for aggressively pursuing the city to comply with the conditions of the park land donation (see pages 54-55).

The economy was healthy in 1907, but most importantly, Manito Park was ready to receive its neighborhood. To describe the building atmosphere around Manito Park, the following is a sampling of Grinnell's 1907 advertising campaign taken from various issues of *The Spokesman-Review:*

The Isaac N. Peyton home at Eighth and Grand, along the route to Montrose (Manito) Park, circa 1885. The boys on the horses are Horace and Harlan. The water tower in the background is in the vicinity of the present-day reservoir. (Photo MAC L94-40.41)

The Manito Grocery, 3003 South Grand Avenue, in 1907.
(Photo courtesy Spokane Public Library, Northwest Room)

MANITO

No section of the city, aside from the business section, is contributing so much toward the development of a Greater Spokane as the Manito residence section. This statement is not based on our opinions nor on the opinion of any person, but it is based on facts and figures which cannot be disputed. Figures sometimes lie, or a least can be made to deceive, but facts prove the statement.

No Other District But Manito Is Free From the Railroad Danger, We Now Have an Automobile in Which to Show You Around

The Manito residence section is known as one of the most desirable residence sections in the city.

The Way Is Made Easy For You

You will never have a better opportunity to secure a home site than today. We let you name your own terms, and Manito property is selling at the present time below its actual value. Only a small cash payment required and you can tell us how you want to pay the balance. Band concert at the park today. Come out. We have opened a new branch office at the park on Manito Place. We have another office at Twenty-ninth and Grand and will have carriages at both in which to show you around.

Some Facts About Manito

10 miles of cement sidewalks.
62 houses now under construction.
1600 shade trees planted along the streets.
$35,000 spent in the public park
12 miles of graded street
207 houses completed in 3 years
7 miles of water mains laid
Several miles of gas mains laid.

THE "MANITO KIND"
Of Home Site Is Not Found Elsewhere

In no other part of the city are there such beautiful surroundings as at Manito. The principal park of the city, consisting of 95 acres; the [Spokane] Country Club, which has beautiful grounds and buildings; Manito boulevard, which is to be the show street of the city; the campus and buildings of the new Spokane College [on 29th Avenue near Grand Boulevard] and the new Rosedale boulevard, which is soon to be constructed, all surround Manito.

In addition to the beautiful surroundings, the building restrictions assure the Manito residence section will always be beautiful. Then, too, no railroads can ever reach Manito. It is way above them. Manito is favored with everything that could be desired for a residence section.

At Manito Park Tonight

You will find a free moving picture exhibition. Every night, Sunday excepted, there is a free moving picture exhibition in the park. There is also a free lecture, illustrated by the stereopticon, which is not only entertaining but highly instructive.

Manito is the Coolest Spot in Town

Come out this evening and enjoy the free moving picture exhibition between 8 and 9 o'clock. It is delightfully cool and you will have an enjoyable time.

Every day now is a picnic day at Manito. Take a trip to Manito any evening about 6 o'clock and in the park you will find from 50 to 100 or more families eating their suppers in the cool, open air; the coolest spot in Spokane; from 10 to 15 degrees cooler than it is in the downtown districts. If your home is in the Manito district you do not need to go to the mountains for the summer. You have the mountain air at your home.

For Soil For Their Flowers the Ladies Go to Manito

Some of the richest and blackest soil in the city is to be found at Manito. It is the kind of soil that makes it easy for you to have a beautiful yard; combined with the soil are the artistic boulders and fine pines, all of which are making the South Side Hill section the most beautiful residence section.

Inferior or Superior Quality
Which Do You Want in Your Home Site Providing
It Is Just as Easy to Secure One as the Other?

We believe that you want a home site which has superior qualities; one that is located in a part of the city which will never have any but fine residences; a home site that will grow in value as the city develops; a home site that contains the artistic features that will make it desirable; a home site located in that section of the city which contains more public improvements than any other part – in short – the kind of home site you find at MANITO.

Not a commonplace section, but a section where the homes of all are up to the high standard for which better residence sections of Spokane have become noted. A section where improvements precede the erection of the homes.

MANITO
THE REASON WHY

Read this extract from an article in the Spokesman-Review of July 14th [1907]: "It is the natural tendency of residence districts to seek the high points overlooking the city. There is also a rugged picturesqueness embodied in the boulders and pine trees in much of the South Side property that appeals to the homebuilder. Then there is an unevenness in the lay of the ground which gives variety and puts most of the lots above street grades, which is an attractive feature. These are some of the 'characteristics' of South Side additions on the hill which probably cause the property to command higher prices than in most North Side Additions."

MANITO HAS NO COMPETITORS

Manito stands in a class by itself as a high class residence district! There are many reasons:

FIRST – Manito is naturally the choice residence section, being built on the South Side, above the city and the railroads and commanding a magnificent view. These are qualities which make the finest residence districts in all cities.

SECOND – The building restrictions have been enforced and none but nice residences have been erected.

THIRD - The owners of Manito Addition have spared no expense in the matter of improvements and today Manito is ahead of many districts not as far out, having good streets, cement sidewalks and city water.

FOURTH – Purchasers of Manito lots have been treated right. No unfair advantages have been taken and they have been given more for their money than buyers in any other part of the city. Manito has grown faster than any section of the city and more money has been spent there than in any other one section. All of the houses at Manito are new. Wouldn't you rather build in such a section than where the development has reached its height?

BY ACTUAL COUNT

62

Houses Are Under Construction at

Manito Park

JUST STOP AND THINK A MINUTE WHAT THIS MEANS: Over $150,000 being spent for houses that are under course of construction within the boundaries of Manito Park addition today. By the way, that does not include the large number of houses that have already been completed at Manito this year.
Is there any other addition in the city with such a record? None that any one has heard of!

Where the most fine homes are being built is the place for you to build

Name your own terms on a Manito lot. We will do the rest.

The Fred B. Grinnell Company

TERMINAL BUILDING.   PHONE 728.

Manito Office, Twenty-ninth and Grand.

**An advertisement from the
July 13, 1907 Spokesman-Review.**

HISTORY REPEATS ITSELF
Spokane Is No Exception To The Rule

The history of all cities in this and other countries is that the finest residence districts ultimately seek the higher levels. In Spokane the highest level is at MANITO.

It is the natural outcome of the development of any city of any size for the best residence district to be on the hill sections. The railroads, the business houses and manufactories must of necessity be located on the lower levels and as time goes on and a city develops the "one-time" best residences give place to business houses. Every resident of Spokane has implicit faith in the development of the city and believes that within a few years it will be one of the important cities of the country. When that belief has been fulfilled where will the choice residence section be? Being elevated 350 feet above Howard and Riverside, Manito benefits by the prevailing warm southwesterly winds and is entirely free from the winter fogs and dampness experienced at intervals in the lower districts of the city.

The previous pages describe the crux of the advertising information disseminated to the public during the peak growth years of the Manito area. The most active years of development and housing construction on the Manito plateau spanned from 1907 until the Depression years of the 1930s.

Many of the springs throughout Manito Park now feed into the duck pond. This was the first spring house, encrusted with ice, in the future park site. *(Photo MAC L94-57.87)*

The Glover Block, pictured here in 1883, was Herman Preusse's first architectural commission in Spokane. It was located at the southwest corner of Front (now Spokane Falls Boulevard) and Howard Street. The wagon train belonged to George Mitchell and was loading supplies for the military Fort Spokane. (Photo courtesy Jerome Peltier)

The upscale areas of early Spokane, especially during the "Age of Elegance," were designed with a strong European influence. Both of Spokane's earliest and most prominent architects came from Germany. Herman Preusse was born in Germany in 1847. When he was three years old, his father died and his mother married one of Germany's leading architects. Under his influence, Preusse received one of the finest architectural educations in Germany. Drawing on the experience and education he received in his stepfather's office, he gained early recognition as one of Germany's upcoming young architects.

Herman Preusse
(Spokane and the Inland Empire, N.W. Durham)

Drawn by promising opportunities in America, a young and booming nation, Preusse moved to New York in 1870. Following a number of successful career moves in the United States, he settled in Spokane Falls in 1882. In 1887, Preusse hired Julius Zittel. Zittel was only 18 years of age, but within six years, his talents and skill led to a partnership with Preusse. The partnership lasted for 18 years. They designed and supervised the construction of some of the finest buildings in Spokane, including Gonzaga College, St. Aloysius Catholic Church, the Carnegie Library, and Auditorium Theatre. Preusse was the first professional architect in Spokane, and one of four architects listed in the *1888 Spokane Falls Directory.* By 1906 there were over forty listed. Some of the most prominent designed houses for the newly-developing Manito area.

Julius Zittel
(Spokane and the Inland Empire, N. W. Durham,)

Kirtland K. Cutter, Spokane's most famous architect, was born in Cleveland, Ohio, in 1860. His father, a banker with the Merchant's National Bank of Cleveland, provided young Cutter with a comfortable lifestyle. However, he was greatly influenced by his great grandfather, Professor Jared Kirtland, while living at Kirtland's country estate. A well-connected and respected naturalist, Kirtland socialized with many of the nation's notable people. This period of Cutter's life appears to have given him a high degree of sophistication and confidence. Cutter studied painting and sculpture at the Art Students League in New

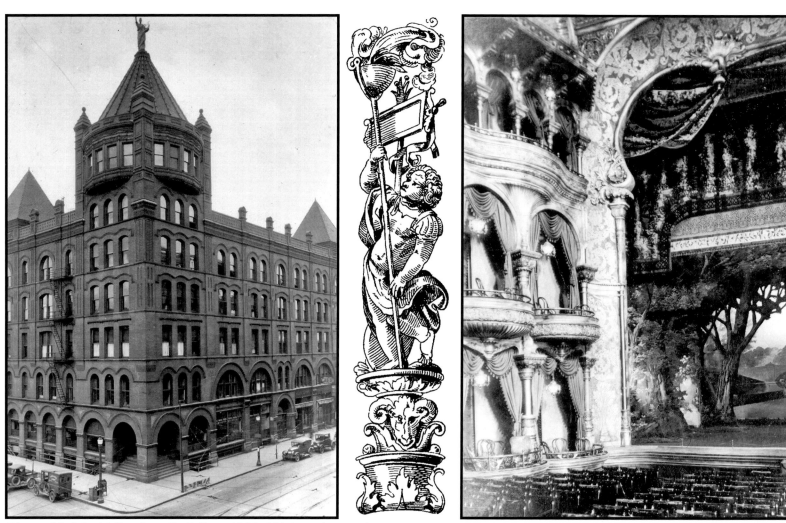

The red brick Auditorium Building, 1890-1934, at the northwest corner Main and Post, and an interior shot of its theater (right). It was designed by Herman Preusse and financed by Anthony M. Cannon and John J. Browne. (Photo courtesy Jerome Peltier)

York. He then spent several years traveling and studying in Europe. Upon Kirtland's return to the United States, his uncle Horace Cutter, a banker in Spokane Falls, convinced the younger Cutter to join him there. It does not appear that Cutter's training included any formal education in the field of architecture, but he had an ability to visualize beautiful designs and transfer them to paper. He was a talented illustrator and, through his travels, had been exposed to a wide variety of architectural designs, from which he developed his own unique eclectic style. His enthusiasm, charming sophistication, and connections to wealthy and influential individuals (contacts acquired primarily through his Uncle Horace) would become contributing factors to his eventual international fame.

Spokane experienced a devastating fire on August 4, 1889. The fire decimated most of the downtown business district, consuming 25 city blocks and destroying 60 brick and stone buildings (about half of these buildings were large commercial structures referred to at the time as "blocks"). The fire created an opportunity for Cutter's architecture practice to flourish (along with everyone else's involved in the reconstruction of Spokane).

A previous fire, which occurred in 1883, also affected the future of Spokane's architecture. It signaled a need for brick construction. In his book *Spokane and the Inland Empire*, Nelson Durham states:

The first considerable fire which left its mark in Spokane startled the city on the night of January 19, 1883. The conflagration broke out the coldest night of the winter, in the store of F. R. Moore & Co., and as there was no fire department, the space between Front street and the alley south, comprising F. R. Moore & Co.'s store, Charlie Carson's restaurant, Forrest's grocery, Porter's drugstore and the post office, was completely leveled, and Rima's jewelry store across the alley was torn down to arrest the flames. It was a heavy loss and could ill afford to be borne, but the losers had resolved almost before the ashes had cooled down, to rebuild with brick. The year 1883 was thus signalized by a new impetus in building.

Kirtland Cutter
(Spokane Falls and
Its Exposition, *1890)*

Karl Malmgren
(Spokane Falls and Its
Exposition, *1890)*

Riverside Avenue, looking east, following Spokane's devastating fire of August 4, 1889. *(Patsy Clark Collection, courtesy Mark Danner)*

One life was lost in the Great Fire of 1889 – George Davis, a civil engineer who jumped out the window in his room at the Arlington Hotel after it caught fire. In terms of lives lost to fires in Spokane, two others hold that record. In 1892, four men were killed during a fire on Havermale Island. The worst fire on record in terms of lives lost occurred January 26, 1898, when the Great Eastern Block burned, killing nine people. The five-story brick building, located at the southeast corner of Riverside and Post, was one of the first business blocks in Spokane. Following the fire, it was rebuilt as the Peyton Building.

An amusing incident of looting took place during the 1889 fire. This was described in the July 5, 1889 issue of the *Daily Chronicle:* "Hall & Noble [undertakers] rolled out a barrel of embalming fluid to the rear of their store during the fire, which was afterwards carried off by somebody. They evidently thinking it to be whiskey."

When Cutter began his business practice as an architect, he formed a partnership with John Poetz, who had been educated in structural design and construction management. Poetz left the firm in 1894 and was replaced by Karl Gunnar Malmgren, who had trained as an architect in his native Sweden. The Cutter-Malmgren partnership lasted about 23 years. To a great extent, Cutter produced the ideas and Malmgren engineered the plans. Although the firm often employed other draftsmen, Malmgren was its key engineer.

Cutter's marriage in 1892 to the daughter of one of Spokane's richest and most influential entrepreneurs helped boost his career. At the age of 32, Kirtland Cutter wed 20-year-old Mary Edwine Corbin, the daughter of Daniel C. Corbin. Following a trip to Europe and an ensuing separation, the marriage ended in divorce on June 30, 1896. In the divorce decree Kirtland alleged his wife refused to return to the United States with him; Mary alleged she was sick and unable to travel, and that he left her in France with no means of support. During their marriage, they had one child, Kirtland Corbin Cutter. A strained relationship between D.C. Corbin and Kirtland Cutter resulted from the divorce. Corbin was instrumental in keeping Cutter's son from him, and insisted his grandson's name be changed

Kirtland K. Cutter's residence, a Swiss-style chalet that he called Chalet Hohenstein, at 628 West Seventh Avenue in 1928. Cutter built his home in 1887 and subsequently enlarged and completely remodeled it. Inset is the eight-story steel and concrete condominium at 700 West Seventh Avenue, built on the site of the Cutter home. (Photo MAC L87-1.36501.28)

from Kirtland Corbin Cutter to Corbin Corbin. In one of the provisions of Cutter's will, he states, "I make no provision in this my last Will and Testament for my son, Corbin Corbin, for the reason that his Grandfather, the late D. C. Corbin of Spokane, Washington, in his Will made suitable provision for him on the stipulated condition that his surname be changed to 'Corbin'."

Cutter's most prosperous years began around 1897 and lasted into the early 1900s. During those years, he was the architect of choice for many of the wealthy Spokane families. He designed the majority of the mansions directly below the rim of the Manito plateau ("The Hill"), which were some of his first major commissions.

Cutter experienced some difficult times after his divorce from Mary Corbin. Because of his high profile, on September 4, 1907, *The Spokesman-Review* gave the following detailed account of an embarrassing incident that took place about a year and a half after he married his second wife, society woman Katharine Phillips Williams:

KICKS ARCHITECT OFF STREET CAR
Jack Williams Applies Boot to Kirtland K. Cutter.

Kirtland K. Cutter, society man and architect, whose reputation is national, was kicked from a Manito park car last Thursday evening by "Jack" Williams, society man and former secretary of the Sullivan Mining company, who now has offices with former Judge George Turner in the Fernwell building. Mr. Cutter received the kick as he was descending the steps of the car at Sixth avenue and Washington street, but he landed on his feet when he struck the ground, and after picking up his hat, which fell in the mud, due to his hurried flight, he hastened on his way

to his home without glancing back or making any remarks to his assailant. On account of the social prominence of the two men the occurrence has caused much talk among the members of the Spokane club and the Country club.

Mr. Cutter is married to Mr. Williams' divorced wife, the wedding taking place soon after the divorce was granted ... According to the chronicle of those who saw the melee, it occurred on a Manito park-bound car at 5:40 o'clock last Thursday afternoon. The car was crowded with home-going residents of the hillside and Manito park neighborhoods. Because of the crowded condition of the car and the fact that Mr. Cutter kept going after the kick had been administered most of those on the car were not aware of what had happened. "The first that I knew that trouble had broken out between the erstwhile friends, Cutter and Williams, was when I heard Mr. Williams say, "You __ _ _ __ get off the car," said a wealthy resident of the hill, who was just in the rear of Mr. Williams.

"Then," said the spectator, "Mr. Cutter's hat shot into the air. He followed the hat from the car, never said a word, and ignored the little mishap ... The affair occurred at Sixth avenue and Washington street. It was raining cats and dogs. Cutter thumped his umbrella into position first and then gathered his hat from the mud. He went up Sixth avenue in the direction of his home.

"The affair occurred so quickly that I did not comprehend at the time that a kick had been delivered. Mr. Williams was standing in a crowd on the rear platform of the car and Mr. Cutter had been inside the car... Another friend of Mr. Williams said: "...Jack told me that he had been waiting for a chance to plug Cutter for some time, and this was the first opportunity he had to deliver the chastisement."

Cutter continued to practice architecture in Spokane until 1923. Although his practice extended into other states, most of his work was accomplished in Spokane. When the big money poured into the city in the late 1800s and the wealthy built their elegant mansions, Cutter was able to command a substantial commission for his services. As the demand for these mansions slowed, Cutter found himself in an extremely competitive position. The bottom was falling out of his upscale market and the competition was meeting the demand for more affordable house plans. By the time Cutter left Spokane in 1923, his practice had declined. He went in search of a market compatible with his talents, which he found in Long Beach, California. Kirtland Kelsey Cutter practiced architecture until his death on September 26, 1939, in Long Beach, California, at the age of 79. Cutter's only offspring had one son, also named Corbin Corbin, but who adopted the name "Joe" Corbin. This last Kirtland Cutter descendant, who was born on July 26, 1926, died in Los Angeles on October 13, 1998.

After Manito Park was donated to the city, the surrounding area developed rapidly, although the demand for new home construction began to concentrate in a moderately-priced range. From Spokane's inception until about 1915, the population growth was steady, reaching over 139,000 according to the United States census taken that year. Spokane was a lucrative market for architects. By 1907 eighteen architectural firms were listed in the Spokane directory, many employing numerous architects. A lot of homes built in the Manito area came from these architects' designs. About this time, however, a new concept in house plans emerged – house-plan catalogs.

Catalog plans were largely in response to the popularity of the Craftsman Bungalow, which had received high-profile coverage in various architectural and home design magazines. About 1908 the Ballard Plannery Company was formed. This architectural firm issued a 106-page catalog of house blueprints for minimal costs. A large number of lumber companies operating in Spokane also sold house plans. The catalog plans frequently offered pre-cut packages of lumber and assembly instructions.

When America entered World War I, residential construction slowed. In the decade following 1915, Spokane experienced a temporary downturn in population. Population figures from various sources often conflict, due partially to the expansion occurring beyond Spokane's city limits, which was not included in official census counts. In earlier years, the city limits were more narrowly defined, changing as the city grew. Many of the most rapidly growing areas, such as Hillyard, were not included until later. By 1923, the year of Cutter's departure from Spokane, the housing market was rebounding and Spokane ranked among the top twenty Pacific Coast cities in "the race for leadership in building permits." This statistic was released by the Federal Reserve Bank in March 1924, and appeared in the *Spokane Press* on March 18th. During this period, the Craftsman Bungalow became one of the most popular styles in the Manito area.

The design influence of Preusse, Cutter, and their associates left a lasting mark on Spokane. Many of the homes built in the Manito neighborhood reflect the European influence, a trademark of Spokane's early architects, and are admired by residents today.

The Phoenix Sawmill, at Post Street and the Spokane River, was on the site occupied by Spokane's first sawmill, Scranton-Downing's, built in 1871. The Phoenix mill was in operation from 1898 to 1927. (Photo courtesy Jerome Peltier)

A flatbed truck and trailer for hauling lumber. After the lumber was delivered, the trailer was loaded on the truck to save wear.

An early two-ton GMC lumber truck owned by L. O. Connelly from Aladdin, Washington, loaded for a delivery. (*Above photos courtesy Thelma Shriner*)

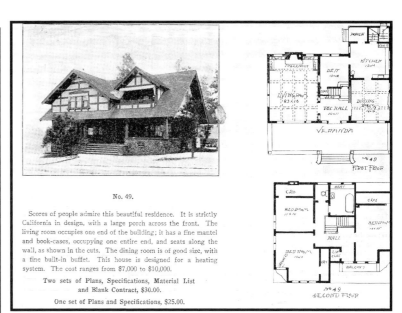

No. 49.

Scores of people admire this beautiful residence. It is strictly California in design, with a large porch across the front. The living room occupies one end of the building; it has a fine mantel and book-cases, occupying one entire end, and seats along the wall, as shown in the cuts. The dining room is of good size, with a fine built-in buffet. This house is designed for a heating system. The cost ranges from $7,000 to $10,000.

Two sets of Plans, Specifications, Material List and Blank Contract, $30.00.

One set of Plans and Specifications, $25.00.

A sample advertisement from the Ballard Plannery Company, Inc. In the early 1900s, many lumber companies began competing with the architects by selling house plans. (*Sample plan courtesy Spokane Public Library, Northwest Room*)

Note the similarity of the Cutter-Malmgren designed home (right) located at 1718 West Ninth Avenue to the Ballard Plannery house above. (*Photo courtesy Linda Yeomans*)

Passengers on rear platform of the Manito trolley pass in front of the Henry J. Kaiser residence at 1115 South Grand Boulevard (just below the present Cathedral of St. John) en route to Manito Park in 1911. *(Photo MAC L89-87)*

Henry Kaiser headed companies responsible for the construction of Boulder, Grand Coulee, and Bonneville dams. He also founded Kaiser Aluminum and invented the Kaiser car. When Kaiser had his home (shown above) built in 1908, *The Spokesman-Review* took special note and printed a lengthy, descriptive article about it in the June 14, 1908 edition, remarking that is was a unique residence with a "roof garden." A portion of the article is included as follows:

HENRY KAISER'S NEW HOME ON GRAND STREET EMBODIES ATTRACTIVE FEATURES. CEMENT AND TILE EXTERIOR
Charming Color Effects in Yellow, Red and Green – Floors Hardwood – Novel Inglenook.

Something wholly unique and original as well as highly attractive has been obtained in the effective design of the residence of Henry J. Kaiser has just completed on the east side of Grand street at the head of Sumner avenue. The house plan is strikingly adapted to the unusual site, which is near to and high above the street, and which commands an exceptionally fine view ... While conforming to no type of architecture, the house embodies features from the Swiss and from the Spanish mission, which are made to harmonize attractively. It is one of the many exclusive designs which Architect W. W. Hyslop has made ... Perhaps the most unique feature of the house, and one which has no counterpart in Spokane, is the roof garden, or open lounging room on the roof, with parapet and port holes and awning stretched above, following the lines of the roof. Effectiveness is added by a cornice of tile extending from the parapet in harmony with the roof design ... The exterior walls of the house are cement, in massive effect ... the main rooms have oak floors and the finish is select fir in green stain ... the entire north end is taken up by an inglenook, containing a large fireplace with massive steel hood ... Separating the dining room and the living room are swinging doors with small panes of opalescent glass ... On the south wall is a row of French windows ...

Chapter 6

The Gardens, the Zoo, the Fun

At the time of Francis Cook's acquisition in 1884 of what is now Manito Park, a natural beauty permeated that entire area. The region, in its early days of Spokane's settlement, has been described in many ways, some of which were not flattering, referring to it as an "undeveloped tangle" or a "wooded tangle of underbrush and basaltic rock piles as big as houses." However, its natural beauty appealed to Cook and he initiated the beginnings of the park, which he advertised in the *Spokane Falls Review*. One of the earliest and most complete descriptions of it appeared on April 21, 1888:

MONTROSE PARK!

An elevated plateau adjoining the city; affording the finest residence sites. It has broad avenues, shade trees, abundance of water and is traversed by the motor line. It commands fine views and lies within five minutes ride of the heart of the city.

THE SITE IS BEAUTIFUL; HEALTHY AND ATTRACTIVE!
The property in this suburban park is offered to purchasers at low figures and on easy terms; Apply to **Northwestern Land Company,** *Spokane National Bank Building, for particulars.*

MONTROSE PARK
Among the many new additions adjoining the City of Spokane Falls, none have so fully met with all the requirements of a first-class residence site as Montrose Park; which will be placed on the market on **Monday, April 23**.

It lies south of the city, and comprises a portion of the beautiful plateau overlooking the valley of the Spokane. This plateau as it now appears presents to the appreciative eye a

SYLVIAN [sic] PARADISE
The open woody stretches of gently undulating ground afford elegant residence sites, and will be occupied ere long with many bright and happy homes. Besides the natural attractions that offer there are wide avenues of one hundred and twenty feet. This will give twenty feet for promenades on each side with an eighty foot driveway. Plenty of water can be had upon this upper level at from twenty to forty feet in depth. In some portions of this addition fine springs abound. To further and to the desirability of Montrose Park, there will be three fine parks laid out with fine drives and walks and some will contain miniature lakes and fountains. Wherever one finds wild roses the soil where they grow is sure to be rich and strong. Scattered about on the gentle slopes and the pretty open plazas wild roses bloom in great profusion--hence the name--"**MOUNTAIN OF ROSES!**"

The present Manito duck pond, formerly called Mirror Lake, as it appeared in its pristine state around 1925. Over the years, numerous changes have been made to the pond's surrounding vegetation. The spring-fed pond is much smaller today than it was at the time of the park's inception. (Photo courtesy Spokane Parks and Recreation Department)

This new addition comprises six hundred acres and lies only twelve blocks from Riverside avenue. The new motor line traverses the new addition on three broad avenues, and thus the remotest portions of Montrose will be within five minutes ride of the heart of the city. That which also adds to the desirability of Montrose Park for residence sites is the healthfulness of location. The mean elevation above the business portion of the city is 350 feet. This places it above the fog line and where one gets the benefit of the southern breezes and the sun. At many points it commands fine views. The streets are easy to construct and will be comparatively inexpensive.

Purchasers will receive a satisfactory guarantee for the completion of the motor line through the property, and which guarantee will form a part of the Contract Of Purchase. Call and see plat and get particulars.

The following excerpt from the same newspaper describes the excitement and anticipation of the completion of the Spokane & Montrose Railroad to Cook's development and the beauty of the area:

Our citizens will rejoice when they can be carried quickly and cheaply to the shady groves and sparkling fountains of Montrose Park. No one will be credited with having seen Spokane hereafter unless he has ridden over its heights on the Spokane & Montrose railroad ... This will be the route for all local picnics and family excursions. The elevated property south of the business portion of the city will now come to the front as the healthiest and most fashionable residence section.

Another description of the Montrose area was in a report to the City of Spokane by the Olmsted Brothers, a nationally renowned landscape architectural firm from Brookline, Massachusetts, which designed parks and private gardens in many major cities. Frederick Law Olmsted, the patriarch of the family who had founded the firm, was one of the designers of Central Park in New York City. On July 10, 1907, at a cost of $1000 plus expenses, the park board hired the Olmsted firm to prepare a preliminary recommendation for Spokane's existing parks and to assist in the development of an overall park and boulevard system. Following an inspection of Manito Park, they stated:

The city is fortunate in possessing already a local park so large, so well situated, and accessible as this is ... The picturesque, weather-beaten ledges, especially interesting to city people used to tidy, clipped lawns and grass plots, appear to be in process of being gradually covered over with a thin layer of earth followed by grass ... There is much rough, ledgy ground in this park. Doubtless that had something to do with its selection for a park. The land, that is to say, looked discouraging for low-priced suburban lots. In some degree it is discouraging and costly to fit it for use as a public park, yet it is worth more for a park than fifty-foot lots ... The prominent ledges are decidedly valuable as picturesque landscape features. They should be carefully preserved and taken advantage of in designing all kinds of improvements.

The Olmsted report detailed their impression of the infant park in 1907. The nearly two-page narrative on Manito recommended future improvements. A third of the report was devoted to the zoo at Manito, primarily recommending its removal. (It was removed 25 years later during the Depression, but purely for economic reasons.) Manito Park did not develop from a master plan, but has been a constantly evolving, changing environment, shaped primarily by the inspiration or vision

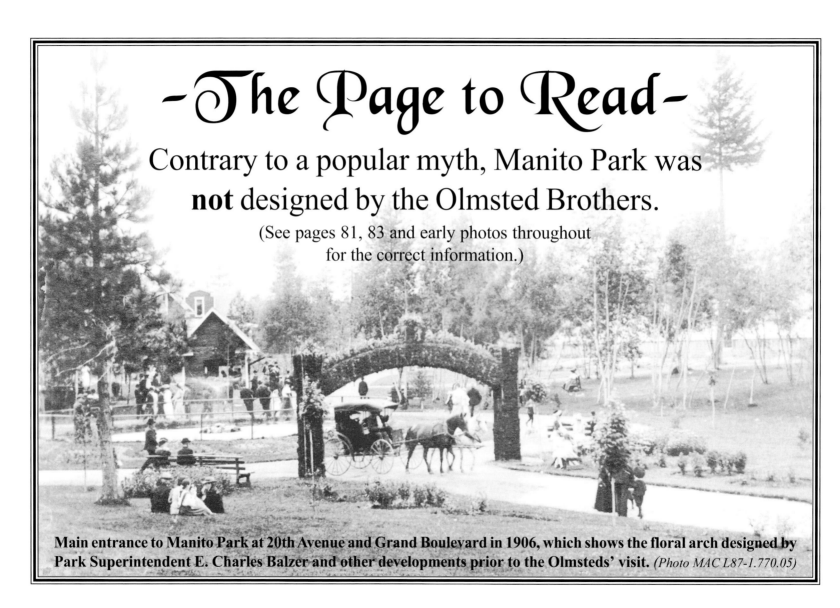

-The Page to Read-

Contrary to a popular myth, Manito Park was **not** designed by the Olmsted Brothers.

(See pages 81, 83 and early photos throughout
for the correct information.)

Main entrance to Manito Park at 20th Avenue and Grand Boulevard in 1906, which shows the floral arch designed by Park Superintendent E. Charles Balzer and other developments prior to the Olmsteds' visit. *(Photo MAC L87-1.770.05)*

of various park superintendents or directors. There is a popular mistaken notion, largely perpetuated by a park department brochure published some years ago, that Manito Park was an Olmsted Brothers' design. Even the content of the Olmsted report describing the existing layout confirms they did not design Manito Park.

Eventually some of the Olmsted Brothers' recommendations were implemented: park roads were widened, paved and grades reduced; an open area was graded for a level playing field; and continuous grassy areas were planted. Few specific landscape suggestions were offered, except to add another 31 acres to remove irregular boundaries, which they felt were not conducive to pleasing park design. That suggestion never materialized.

At the time Manito Park was donated to the city, the parks were governed by politics and park donors. A special charter in 1891 had placed Spokane's public parks under joint supervision of the mayor, city engineer and city council president, subject to the authority of the city council. In 1955 the Eastern Washington State Historical Society taped an interview with Laurence R. Hamblen and Joel E. Ferris, who discussed the Spokane park system history. Hamblen and Ferris were both civic-minded citizens with long-term service to the park commission. Hamblen, then-president of the Spokane Park Board and board member since 1912, explained Spokane's early governing body, as follows, "At that time, Spokane was governed by a council of ten members, two from each ward in the city. The city, of course, was divided into five wards. This meant that the full system was largely political because each ward wanted to acquire for its constituents more than the other wards. The result was a political issue all of the time."

As previously noted, many Spokane parks were donated by owners of nearby property who clearly understood the potential benefit of having the city improve the park land. A front page article in the August 4, 1907 *Spokesman-Review* stated:

Park Improvements Add Fifteen Times Their Cost to Adjacent Property *– Property adjacent to a developed boulevard is 100 per cent more valuable than it would have been in the same district without the park or boulevard improvements having been made. This is the unanimous opinion of real estate men, who are in one accord in boosting for a better park and boulevard system ...*

In an attempt to remove the parks from the political arena and protect against exploitation by park donors, a 1907 charter amendment created a separate nonpartisan park board commission of ten unpaid members, with the mayor serving as an ex officio member. Another amendment in 1910 eliminated the mayor's position and provided for a city council representative to act as a liaison between the city and the park board.

Correspondence and park board minutes filed in the Eastern Regional State Archives and the Spokane Parks and Recreation Department archives provide insight into the formation of the Spokane Parks Department. The founding of the park board was largely through the efforts of Aubrey Lee White and the Spokane Chamber of Commerce, of which White was director. Although Spokane was surrounded by open country and had little need to preserve land for parks, with the city's rapid growth and expansion, White had the foresight to push for preservation of open space while it was still available and affordable. He organized and served as president of the City Beautiful Club,

Aubrey Lee White (1869-1948) and his wife Ethelyn (Binkley) with daughters Mary, Elizabeth (Betty), Louise and baby Harriet.

Left: Aubrey and Ethelyn (seated center) White and their daughters, from left, Mary (Mrs. Henry) Hart, Dr. Elizabeth (Betty) White, Harriet (Mrs. Calhoun) Shorts and Louise (Mrs. William) Willis. Right: Aubrey and Ethelyn White's grandson Charles Willis (Louise's son), his wife Melissa and their sons Herald and Winfield, circa 1985. (All photos this page courtesy Charlie Willis)

created to promote the establishment of a city park and playground system that would put a park or recreation area within walking distance of every neighborhood. The initial park board was comprised of businessmen with common interests. Aubrey White was chosen as the first president of the board, serving from 1907 to 1922. His determination to secure a viable park system for Spokane took tangible form soon after the park board was formed. Grading, seeding and planting of Manito Boulevard began and, within three years, a $1,000,000 park bond was passed to expand and improve the park system. As park funds were limited, White persuaded private citizens to plant many of the deciduous trees that beautify Spokane's streets today. His foresight and tireless campaign to secure public park lands earned White the reputation as "Father of Spokane's Park System."

In addition to his unflagging park-promotion endeavors, Aubrey White was also active in numerous business ventures. He was in partnership with Jay P. Graves in the Old Ironside and Granby mining properties. He was also involved in Graves's railway lines (Spokane Traction Company, Coeur d'Alene Electric Railway, and Spokane & Inland Railway Company) and participated in the reorganization of the three companies into the Inland Empire Railway Company, of which Graves was the president and White vice-president. White, Graves and several other investors (the Spokane-Washington Improvement Co.), owned large tracts of land, including some land donated for Manito Park. Although White had numerous conflicts of interest, his connections and influence were driving forces behind Spokane's development. White's memory has been honored by the naming of the Aubrey L. White Parkway in Riverside State Park, and the preservation of an area he loved along the Little Spokane River as a park.

The original officers and directors of the Spokane River Parkway Association, from left: W. G. Merryweather, W. M. Burns, John W. Duncan, W. H. Farnham, George W. Dodds, Aubrey L. White, W. S. McCrea, Charles Hebberd and R. J. Martin.
(Frank W. Guilbert photo courtesy Charlie Willis.)

Aubrey Lee White's Famous Heritage

Aubrey White was a direct descendant of William and Suzanna White, who were among the 102 *Mayflower* passengers to set foot in America on November 11, 1620, at present-day Provincetown, Massachusetts. Their son Peregrine White was born on the *Mayflower* while anchored in the harbor. William died shortly after their arrival and, a few months later, Suzanna married Edward Winslow, whose wife also died that first winter. Theirs was the first English marriage in the New England colonies. Suzanna and Edward's son, Josiah Winslow, became the first governor of the colony born on U.S. soil.

The first newspaper reference to activity at Manito Park, subsequent to the 1903 announcement that land was to be donated, was in *The Spokesman-Review* on December 23, 1903: "Mayor Boyd says the grove will be cleaned up, grass sowed and the dancing platform put in shape to make it an ideal picnic ground." For years prior to its first appearance in the *Polk Directory* in 1900, Montrose Park had been a popular destination for recreational outings. As referenced earlier, newspaper accounts place the first Spokane County fair in this area, as well as it being the destination of Francis Cook's first motorized trolley trip to the Manito plateau. By all indications, Montrose Park was much smaller than the new Manito Park and primarily encompassed the area of the present picnic grounds at the 18th Avenue entrance and the duck pond.

This grove, photographed in 1910, in Manito Park may be the one referenced in the news account cited above. (Photo courtesy Bill Stewart)

Spokane's first park superintendent was E. Charles Balzer, a German-born immigrant who was employed as the "city florist" in 1900, at the age of 23. According to a *Spokeman-Review* article following Mr. Balzer's death on December 6, 1953, he had studied horticulture, park development and rose culture in Germany and France before coming to the United States. He worked for the park department in St. Louis, Missouri, before coming to Spokane. In 1902 he became the first park superintendent.

E. Charles Balzer, circa 1935, founder of the Balzer Nursery and the first Spokane park superintendent. (Photo courtesy the Balzer family)

Because park records were not kept until the park board was formed in 1907, information regarding the operation of the early park system is sketchy. Much of Balzer's correspondence from 1907 to 1909 is at the Washington State Archives, Eastern Region. Most of it was written on official letterhead stationary inscribed with: "**E. C. BALZER, Superintendent of City Parks,** Residence: Manito Park, Phone Main 4817." This same letterhead also lists the city parks: Manito, 93 acres; Liberty, 23 acres; Corbin, 13-1/2 acres; Coeur d'Alene, 10 acres; Audubon 33 acres; and Stadacona, 1-1/2 acres.

Faced with the task of developing this large park, the city moved its greenhouses from Liberty Park to Manito in October of 1904. They were situated just inside the main entrance of the park at 20th Avenue,

*Main entrance to Manito Park at 20th and Grand in 1906. The floral arch over the entrance, designed by Park Superin-
tendent Charles Balzer, was covered with multicolored ivy trained into the words "See Spokane Shine." The arch was
removed in 1909. To the left of the arch in the background was Balzers' residence and concession stand. The greenhouses, moved from Liberty Park in 1904, are barely visible behind the trees at the far right.* (Photo MAC L87-1.770.05)

A family outing at Manito Park in the early 1900s. *(Photo courtesy Spokane Public Library, Northwest Room)*

about 300 feet west of Grand Boulevard (see photo previous page). Charles Balzer would be concentrating his time at Manito. Spokane Park Board minutes covering the early years of Manito Park reflect regular correspondence from Fred Grinnell – the real estate broker representing the park donors, who held the majority of property for sale around the park – reminding the park board of their obligations.

By the time the park board was formed, Balzer was in charge of all the city parks. His experience as city florist – and lack of other qualified candidates – made him the natural choice for park superintendent. With the growing demands at Manito Park, a superintendent's house was built in the park near the greenhouses

(in the vicinity of the present Washington Monument). This house was a source of some controversy. In a letter to Mayor Floyd L. Daggett on February 28, 1906, Will Graves, on behalf of Spokane-Washington Improvement Co., referred to "... an unsightly barn of a house now being built in Manito Park ... for the keeper of the greenhouse." He suggested it be removed and "an artistic house built in its place." Apparently this letter was not heeded; when John Duncan was hired in 1910 as the next superintendent, he addressed a letter to the park board in which he said, "In looking over the house for the Superintendent I find it entirely inadequate for such a purpose." He was given a monthly housing allowance of $35, and moved into a home at 2504 S. Manito Boulevard, where he and his wife, Fanny, lived for the remainder of their lives. In 1912 the old superintendent's house was torn down and grass planted.

During Balzer's early years as superintendent, rapid changes took place in Manito Park attracting visitors by the thousands. People dressed in their Sunday attire, packed a picnic basket and gathered up the children to spend a day at the park. Beautiful flower gardens and floral sculptures adorned the park, and a growing zoo captured the attention of young and old alike. B. J. Weeks and the Balzers each had a concession stand with the usual popcorn, ice cream, soda pop, candy, peanuts – and lots of cigars! (After the park department took over the concessions in 1910, its monthly costs during the summer averaged $50 on cigars that were then sold for a nickel a piece.) Regular weekend band concerts and baseball games entertained the picnickers. Money was tight, but Charles Balzer crafted swing sets and other playground equipment out of old power poles, which kept the children happy. By 1913 men enjoyed lawn

The dance pavilion on the southern shore of Mirror Lake (the present duck pond) around 1907. The lake was much larger than today's duck pond. (Photo from a 1907 brochure, MAC L93-31.3)

bowling on the new bowling green. Tennis was so popular that in 1912 a second set of tennis courts were added to the park near the softball field (the first courts, at 17th and Grand, were built in 1908). When the sun set, there were open-air motion pictures projected onto thin sheeting (to be seen from either side) and dancing at the pavilion, situated along the southern shore of Mirror Lake. The lake cooled many swimmers on hot days. On the 4th of July, fireworks displays attracted even larger crowds. In 1912 John Duncan reported to the park board, "A conservative estimate of the number of people there [on July 4th] would be from 15,000 to 20,000...." Even on a quiet day, Manito Park was a popular destination to get away from it all and enjoy nature's beauty.

Flowery path in the old-fashioned garden (now the Joel E. Ferris Perennial Garden) in Manito Park in the early 1920s. (Photo MAC L95-111-205)

Young people relaxing in the park, circa 1907. Situated on the hill just above the people is an elephant topiary (see an enlarged version of it on the opposite page). (Photo MAC L86-30.1)

A better view of the elephant topiary (see photo at left) at Manito Park, circa 1907. (Photo courtesy Bill Stewart)

Charles Balzer built the first playground equipment from old power poles. The play area was located in the general vicinity of the new (1998) one built near the picnic shelter. The park's second play area (above, circa 1903) was near the main 20th and Grand entrance. Another playground was established at the park's south end in 1912. *(Photo MAC, detail of L98-40.3)*

John Duncan, second park superintendent, introduced lawn bowling to Spokane in 1913. An old English-type bowling green was constructed near the upper playground and softball field in Manito Park. (Photo courtesy Spokane Parks and Recreation Dept.)

Regular weekly band concerts in the bandstand, pictured here the year after it was built in 1908, attracted large crowds. It was located at the peak of the hill northeast of the present Park Bench Cafe, which is located at the intersection of Tekoa Street and Loop Drive. It was torn down in 1946. (Libby Studio photo, MAC 2309)

Park visitors enjoying a baseball game at the 19th Avenue and Grand Boulevard entrance to Manito Park in 1907. The water tower, visible to the north, was built to fulfill a condition by the park donors that the city provide a water system for the park and the surrounding real estate development. Francis Cook's house is barely visible to the right of the tower. The homes pictured along Grand were built between 1903 and 1906. (Photo courtesy Spokane Public Library, Northwest Room)

This photo, taken near Grand Boulevard around 1905, shows an unusual garden for this region of the country. The cactus and succulents were undoubtedly moved into the greenhouse in the winter. At the time, the greenhouses were located near the park entrance at 20th Avenue and Grand. (Photo MAC L94-24.83)

a cave seven feet deep, which they covered with boards. One day Mr. Balzer followed his son to the hideout and, to the senior Balzer's delight, discovered the boys had dug into rich, dark soil – perfect topsoil. With much of Spokane's soil being very poor and rocky, Balzer recognized its value and began using this soil for the Manito gardens. Neighbors would also come to take the rich earth home for their own gardens. According to Norb Balzer, in an April 18, 1968 article in the *Spokane Daily Chronicle*, "Eventually he had hauled out 42,500 loads of loam to parks all over the city." As a result, the present level of Duncan Gardens is now much lower than it had originally been, giving it its first name – the Sunken Gardens.

E. Charles and Mathilda Balzer came to Spokane in 1900 from St. Louis, Missouri, where he worked for the park department. He was hired as Spokane's city florist and, in 1902, as the first park superintendent. The Balzers had four children: Norb, Edward, Walter and Elsie. (Photo courtesy the Balzer family.)

Sections of Manito have always been left in a natural "undeveloped" state, which appeals to the adventurer in all young children. During Balzer's early years as superintendent, his young son Norb, with some friends, found the present-day Duncan Gardens an enticing place to play their games. The area was covered with fir and pine trees and the boys needed a good hideout. They proceeded to dig

Balzer Nursery delivery truck. The signs on the truck advertise "tree roses, shrubbery, all kinds of fertilizer and black dirt." (Photo courtesy the Balzer family)

A bird's-eye perspective of the portion of the zoo at the intersection of Tekoa, Manito Place and Loop Drive showing the duck pond with the swan house, monkey cage (far right) and Owl Castle (upper right) in 1905. (Libby Studio photo, MAC L87-1.771.04.)

In 1905 Charles Balzer began acquiring animals for a fledgling zoo in the park. The first residents were beaver and muskrats, located at the present Manito duck pond. Within a short time, the zoo grew into a major attraction. At times it contained as many as 165 various animals. Among the animals at the zoo were bear, elk, deer, monkeys, buffalo, mountain lions, coyotes, foxes, badgers, bob cats, skunks, goats, kangaroos, beavers, muskrats and numerous species of birds. The zoo covered nearly a third of the park.

The park's center of activity was at the present intersection of Tekoa, Loop Drive and Manito Place. From that intersection, facing north around 1910, visible in front and to the left would be a little fenced pond (one of four naturally occurring, spring-fed ponds in the park).

In the pond was an island, on which the "swan house" provided shelter for numerous species of waterfowl. Beyond that, the bear cages nestled up against the rock formations behind the present Park Bench Cafe. (In 1923, this duck pond was filled in to build the cafe.) Looking directly left, one would have seen the monkey cages in the foreground, and in the distance (on what is now Rose Hill), the elk and deer barn. Atop the hill directly behind this position in the intersection was the aviary – the Owl Castle. The Brotherhood of Owls donated the first owl. Straight ahead in the distance, the United States flag blew in the wind up on flag hill. To the right, on the hill above the pond was an array of beautiful gardens, with a topiary of the Masonic Lodge emblem as its centerpiece. On the next hill north, the bandstand was at a perfect location to broadcast the music over the activity below.

Clockwise from top left: Looking northeast in 1909 from the intersection of Loop Drive, Tekoa Street and Manito Place toward Flag Hill, where the flag was hoisted atop a 120-foot pole. The bandstand is at the far right. (Photo courtesy Bill Stewart); ***The same intersection, looking southeast, showing the Owl Castle aviary (top of photo), the swan house on the duck pond island and the bear cages (along the bottom of photo).*** (Photo MAC L94-57-50); ***The same intersection in 1998. The only remaining "land-mark" is the house on the corner.*** (Bamonte photo); ***The Owl Castle aviary in 1905.*** (Photo courtesy Bill Stewart)

Looking west from the hill east of the present Park Bench Cafe, circa 1907. A portion of the Owl Castle aviary is visible just left of the topiary in the shape of the Masonic Lodge emblem (in the foreground). In the distance is the elk and deer barn on the present Rose Hill. The round structure to the right is the monkey cage. (Photo courtesy Spokane Parks and Recreation Department)

The present Rose Hill and the area west to the Japanese Garden was the elk and deer enclosure. Portions of the rock wall enclosure in this area still remain. The enclosure extended north to the point where Loop Drive skirts the crest of the hill, encompassing another small pond. Cages for the skunks, coyotes, bobcats and other smaller animals lined the area of the present rock garden bordering the rose garden. Ostrich, emu and kangaroo lived in the area of the present Japanese Garden, and buffalo roamed the current lilac garden.

During the zoo's 28 year history, there were a few incidents of injuries caused by the caged animals. The most serious sent a chill through the community. On July 10, 1923, nine-year-old Elizabeth Harris was feeding bread to the polar bears. One of the bears pulled her right arm into the enclosure and the other, smelling blood, attacked and severed it. Throughout this entire trauma, Elizabeth was remarkably brave. She insisted she was at fault and that no harm be done to the bears. Her wishes were honored. Elizabeth overcame any suggestion of a handicap and lived a normal life (see dedication page).

The zoo had been in existence for over two years when the Olmsted Brothers made their recommendations to the park board in 1907. Had this report been presented prior to the zoo's inception, it is questionable whether Manito Park would have ever had a zoo. The following are excerpts from this report:

For a few years it may continue to be advisable to have the zoological show in Manito Park, but all arrangements in connection with it there should be made with the idea of eventually removing the show to a larger park ... In parks, the zoological collection should always

The bears were always a major attraction at Manito Park. The enclosure, which measured about 60'x300', was nestled up against the rock wall behind the present Park Bench Cafe. *(Photo MAC L95-35.108)*

be regarded merely as an incidental attraction, and it should not be allowed to absorb an undue share of the park appropriation. A complete zoological show is a very expensive affair, particularly in maintenance.

Contrary to the recommendations of this report, the zoo remained a focal point of the park through 1932. Along with the rest of the country, the Parks Department suffered the effects of the Great Depression. The annual cost to feed the animals had risen to $3,000, a cost that strained park budget. In addition, there was the constant concern about the park's potential liability, as well as neighbors'

In the summer of 1930, the Washington State Game Department gave this pair of eight-week-old orphaned cubs to the Manito Zoo. The lively cubs were entertaining and good-natured, but to make room for them, an old bear (said to be cranky) was killed. Bear stew was served at the Salvation Army shortly thereafter. (Photo courtesy Spokane Parks and Recreation Department)

A few of the zoo's occupants during its existence from 1905 to 1932. Today the only remaining evidence of the zoo are remnants of the rock wall enclosure for the deer and elk, some metal bars that supported the bear cages and a metal ring (for tethering the bears while cleaning cages) embedded in the rock wall behind the Park Bench Cafe. (Photos courtesy Spokane Parks & Recreation Dept.)

Feeding deer at Manito Park. *(Photo courtesy the Balzer family)*

complaints about the stench and nightly screeching or howling from the zoo. The zoo's days were numbered, but the park board did not make the decision lightly; some members even argued in favor of closing the greenhouses instead of the zoo. When the issue was finally put to a vote, the zoo lost by a 6-5 vote.

On October 13, 1932, a terse letter from the secretary of the park board was delivered to John Duncan, then park superintendent: "Dear Sir: At the adjourned regular meeting of the Park Board held this date, the Park Superintendent was instructed to dispose of the animals now at the Manito Park Zoo, to the best advantage without cost to the city, prior to January 1st, 1933." As 1933 dawned, the zoo fell quiet. Many of the animals were sold or given to other zoos, and some were released into the wild. But there are Spokane residents, however, who still remember the trauma of hearing gunshots ring out from the zoo, sealing the fate of those animals for which no homes had been found. Many of these animals were preserved by a taxidermist and, for years, stored or displayed at the Cheney Cowles Museum. At one point, Zero, the polar bear who tore Elizabeth Harris's arm from her body, was among the collection. She had met her demise when her mate jumped on her back, breaking her neck.

With the sudden passing of the zoo, the only tangible reminder of the Balzer era was the bandstand (demolished in 1946). However, Charles Balzer had left a legacy – he secured Manito's place in the hearts of the Spokane residents. His contribution could be summarized by a sentence in a 1907 brochure on Manito, prepared by Spokane-Washington Improvement Co. as part of their intensive marketing campaign. It read: "The district now occupied by the city's largest park was but a few years ago a succession of barren ledges, and to the genius of the landscape gardener has fallen the task of bringing beauty from the rough." During Balzer's tenure as park superintendent, his main focus was on Manito Park. Much of what he did was at his own expense and beyond the expected duties. Park records reveal his dedication to Manito; the early photographs attest to his accomplishments. However, the park board wanted more, as indicated by ongoing correspondence. In 1908 Aubrey White, president of the park board, addressed the board with the following letter:

I think we all realize that very excellent work has been done under trying conditions, and yet I think we all can see many mistakes in judgement have occurred and are occurring which will justify at this time certain necessary changes.

The elk pond, circa 1912, was one of four spring-fed ponds at Manito Park in the early 1900s. During the zoo's existence, elk and deer were enclosed in the area now occupied by the Rose Garden, west to the Japanese Garden and north to the crest of the hill overlooking the present duck pond. (Frank Palmer photo, MAC L84-237.1132)

A barn at the Manito Park zoo. *(Photo courtesy the Balzer family)*

Mr. Balzer, our present Park Superintendent, was advanced to that position from City Florist, because he was the only local man available at that time, and this Commission lacked the means to look outside for a properly qualified man....

Mr. Balzer has good recommendations and certificates as a gardener, and his success with plants and flowers has been very satisfactory; therefore as City Florist having charge of the Greenhouse and flower gardens, his service would be valuable to the park department, but he is not an engineer and cannot take the necessary levels nor run his lines when required, neither can he work out his own plans to scale, as such work has been outside of his experience.

I can therefore see at this time the necessity of employing a man as superintendent of parks who is qualified by experience and technical education to do all the planning and laying out of our new development work ...

Following White's advice, the board ordered the Park Improvement Committee to investigate Balzer's work and make a recommendation. On August 6, 1909, the committee reported the following:

The Park Superintendent, Mr. E. C. Balzer, has failed to comply promptly with the orders of this Board and has shown a disposition to evade the spirit of his instructions. We recommend the Secretary be instructed to write Mr. Balzer that the Board insist on prompt and complete compliance with its orders....

Mr. Balzer having undertaken park improvements on his own initiative without consulting your Improvement Committee, we advise him that park improvements outside of maintenance, are under the direction of the Improvement Committee, and orders for such improvements must issue from the Chairman of Improvements direct, through the Secretary of this Board.

In order to enforce discipline without delay, your Improvement Committee requests complete authority to discharge the Park Superintendent and install a temporary Superintendent if, in the opinion of your Committee, the situation makes such action advisable.

Your Improvement Committee recommends that the Board, at an early date, secure the services of a competent Superintendent, with the wages necessary to obtain a man equal to the responsibility and dignity of the position--one who will have the personality requisite to assist the Board in promoting the work of impressing the urgent need of funds for park areas upon our community.

Following the presentation of this report, a motion was made and immediately passed by the board to accept these recommendations and notify Mr. Balzer of their findings. Throughout the previous year, correspondence from the board to Balzer had been of a terse and somewhat demanding nature. Four months after the improvement committee submitted their report, the board called for Balzer's resignation. He submitted it to them on December 23, 1909, as follows, "Gentlemen: I hereby tender my resignation to go into effect on the first of the year or as soon as possible thereafter as Superintendent." Although early news accounts relay a story of a congenial departure from his position, park board correspondence suggests otherwise.

Charles (far left) and Mathilda (third from right) Balzer at Edward and Eleanor (Wosepka) Balzer's wedding reception, held at the home of Charles and Rose (bride's sister, second from right) Hennessey's home in 1938. The bride's father, Albert Wosepka (far right) was the shipping superintendent at McGoldrick Lumber Company. (Photo courtesy the Balzer family)

(Balzer Nursery advertisement courtesy the Balzer family)

Looking east toward Grand Boulevard and the park's original entrance at 20th Avenue, circa 1910. Following Charles Balzer's resignation as the first park superintendent, his family moved to 2015 South Grand, visible at the center of this photo. (Photo courtesy Spokane Parks and Recreation Department)

John Duncan

(Photo courtesy Spokane Parks and Recreation Dept.)

During the time the park board was pushing for Balzer's resignation, Aubrey White met the assistant park superintendent for the Boston parks system, John W. Duncan, at a park convention in Seattle, and they struck up a friendship. On January 3, 1910, White received a telegraph from John Duncan stating "Will accept offer as per letter of the 24th." As prearranged by White, following Duncan's acceptance of the offer to be superintendent of the Spokane park system, he was to report to work "not later than March 1st, 1910."

John Duncan became one of Manito Park's best known figures. He served as Spokane's park superintendent for 32 years, retiring in 1942 at the age of 77. Born in Aberdeen, Scotland, he moved to Boston with his family when he was a boy. He learned the nursery trade from his father. Although White and the Park Board Commission gave the appearances of seeking someone with a technical education to replace Balzer, there is no record in the available archives indicating Duncan had ever received a formal education. After taking over as superintendent, Duncan spent the first couple of years primarily doing maintenance and cultivating a nursery at Manito Park. The nursery bordered the present Duncan Garden to the east. By 1912, it had 212,000 plants, which would be planted in the various city parks. Over the years, the nursery contained assortments of flowering and ornamental trees, shrubs, and various experimental trees and plants.

During Duncan's tenure as superintendent, he made a number of trips to the eastern states to gather ideas from established parks in larger cities. His first was in 1912, a year in which a new wave of changes were made in the park. The old greenhouses and superintendent's house were torn down and new greenhouses built; the upper level at the southern end of the park was graded to create a level ball field, tennis courts, bowling green, and playground (to which a wading pool was added in 1920) and, of greatest interest to Duncan, work began on the formal European-style garden. He transformed the sunken dirt pit into a masterpiece that received national acclaim. In 1941, the year before Duncan's retirement, the park board honored his years of fine service as superintendent by changing the name of the garden from "Sunken" to "Duncan."

Looking north at the Sunken (later Duncan) Garden and the conservatory, circa 1925. The evergreen trees among the flower gardens were planted about 1920. (Tolman photo, MAC L86-219-120)

Sunken Garden, circa 1915. One of the finest contributions Park Superintendent John Duncan made to Manito was the creation of the Sunken Garden. In 1941, shortly before Duncan's retirement, the park board renamed it Duncan Garden in honor of his years of dedicated service. The present garden extends farther south. *(Photo courtesy Bill Stewart)*

This rose garden, circa 1920, was located at the south end of the Sunken Garden (visible at the top right in the photo at the left). The grapevine-covered arbor, built in the early days of the garden's development, was situated near the site of the present Davenport Fountain. The conservatory can be seen at the far right. (Photo courtesy Spokane Public Library, Northwest Room)

The Duncan Garden has undergone numerous transformations over the years, including a major redesign in 1996. Originally it consisted of just a variety of flower beds, which included a rose garden at the south end. Within a few years, evergreen trees and shrubs were planted among the flower beds. The Davenport Memorial Fountain was constructed in 1956 and a reflection pool was added in 1996. The garden's beauty has always provided an attractive backdrop for posed and candid photographs, an ideal place for special events and informal gatherings, and a beautiful place to just take a stroll.

Site of the Duncan Garden fountain that preceded the present Davenport Fountain, circa 1930. *(Photo courtesy Spokane Parks and Recreation Department)*

Two little girls walking along a path in the Duncan Garden, mid-1930s. *(Frank Guilbert photo, MAC L95-111.215)*

Under Duncan's supervision, the lake at Manito Park, called Mirror Lake during the Montrose Park era, also underwent the first of many alterations. The overall effect of these alterations was a reduction in its size to what is now the duck pond. In the early days of the park, the spring-fed lake extended to the edge of Grand Boulevard. The main body of water was at the present site, with a canal extending to the east. This canal would almost dry up in the late summer, leaving an unattractive mosquito-infested swamp. At the west end of the lake, the water would seep onto nearby lots. In 1912, in order to contain the water, a concrete wall founded on bedrock was built along the north and west sides of the lake. Water from nearby springs was also diverted to the lake to keep the water level up. Because of its proximity to the town, the lake had always been a popular place for children to swim, fish or canoe in the summer, and ice skate in the winter. The changes enhanced the lake for those recreational activities. Eventually the channel was filled in, and in 1974 a concrete retaining wall and deck were built along the northeast end. By this time, the lake had long since become a duck pond.

Many changes in the vegetation have taken place around the pond over the years, but as can be seen from early photographs, it has always been a place of beauty, a sparkling jewel in the heart of the Manito neighborhood. Sadly, in November of 1996, a severe ice storm devastated thousands of Spokane's trees. The storm took its toll at Manito – about 70 of the park's trees were lost and many more damaged. Neighbors reacted when the spring clean-up included removing numerous trees along the water's edge. Not all the trees had sustained ice-storm damage; some were already failing and further stressed by the storm. The Parks Department made the difficult decision to remove them all at once. The serene beauty, with the weeping willows hanging over the water, has been severely altered. But, as the old trees were removed, over 90 young replacements were planted, restoring the picturesque setting. The tranquil beauty of the surrounding area and the excitement of watching and feeding the waterfowl attract visitors from dawn to dusk.

John Duncan initiated other changes at Manito Park during his tenure. As previously stated, during this stage of the park's development, he gradually incorporated some of the recommendations from the 1907 Olmsted Brothers' report. When Duncan retired in 1942, he was designated Superintendent Emeritus of the Park System. The park board minutes credited Duncan with "creating one of the finest series of gardens in the country out of barren rocks, lakes and bogs." Following his death on January 21, 1948, at age 83, the minutes again reflected on Duncan's contribution, as follows, "(he) always had an eye to the practical as well as the beautiful."

Harold T. Abbott, who had become the assistant superintendent in 1938, was hired to replace Duncan. Abbott continued in the position until July 31, 1959, when he resigned to accept a teaching position at Washington State University. Among other park developments during his tenure, with the support of the Rose Society, he supervised the creation of the rose garden on the present Rose Hill, an idea conceived and initiated by John Duncan prior to his retirement. Today, the park superintendent responsibilities fall under the administration of the Parks and Recreation Department director and the Manito Park horticulture supervisor, who also is the liaison between the Parks Department and The Friends of Manito.

Mirror Lake (the present Manito duck pond) in the early 1900s. The little footbridge at the left crossed the canal that extended east to Grand Boulevard. *(Photo courtesy Bill Stewart)*

Looking west at the portion of Mirror Lake that extended from the present duck pond to Grand Boulevard. In the summer, the water level would often dry up, and the channel would become stagnant and mosquito infested. It was later filled and is currently a picnic and playground area. (Frank Palmer photo, Peltier Collection, MAC L84-327.1136)

A most frequently recalled memory of the early days at Manito Park is ice skating on the pond. A bonfire usually blazed as children of all ages gathered to skate and mingle with friends. Contests awarded prizes to the best skaters. In 1955 a memorial fireplace was erected, providing a safer place for the fires. Photo circa 1940. (Photo courtesy Spokane Parks and Recreation Department)

In 1926, during the second Indian Congress held in Spokane, these Indians from the Blackfeet Tribe posed for a picture at the Manito pond. Chief Owen Heavy Breast is in the center. The other four are unidentified. (Frank Guilbert photo, MAC L97-13.10)

Manito Park has long been a favorite location to establish memorials. On June 14, 1932, Spokane's Esther Reed Chapter of the Daughters of the American Revolution (DAR) ceremoniously unveiled and dedicated a monument honoring George Washington. The top photos were taken during the ceremony. The women at the right are Mary Margaret Hawes, Mrs. H. E. Rhodehamel, Mrs. A. L. Hawes, regent of the Esther Reed Chapter, Mrs. W. C. Meyer and Mrs. W. H. DuBois. Bottom photo: Steve Gustafson, horticulture supervisor of the park and the Friends of Manito liaison, and Carmen Hagman, Esther Reed regent, during a rededication ceremony of the Washington Monument on July 11, 2001. The Esther Reed Chapter and the Spokane Parks Department financed the repair of the monument after vandals damaged it. *(All photos courtesy Carmen Hagman)*

Mayor Leonard Funk addressing the large crowd that turned out to celebrate the unveiling and dedication of the Washington Monument in Manito Park on June 14, 1932. This monument was presented to the City of Spokane by the Esther Reed Chapter of the DAR on the 32nd anniversary of the chapter's founding. Esther Reed is the oldest DAR chapter in Spokane, having formed just ten years after the DAR was founded in 1890. Because it was chartered on Flag Day (June 14th), it is nationally known as the Flag Chapter. Note the bandstand at the upper right. (Photo courtesy Carmen Hagman)

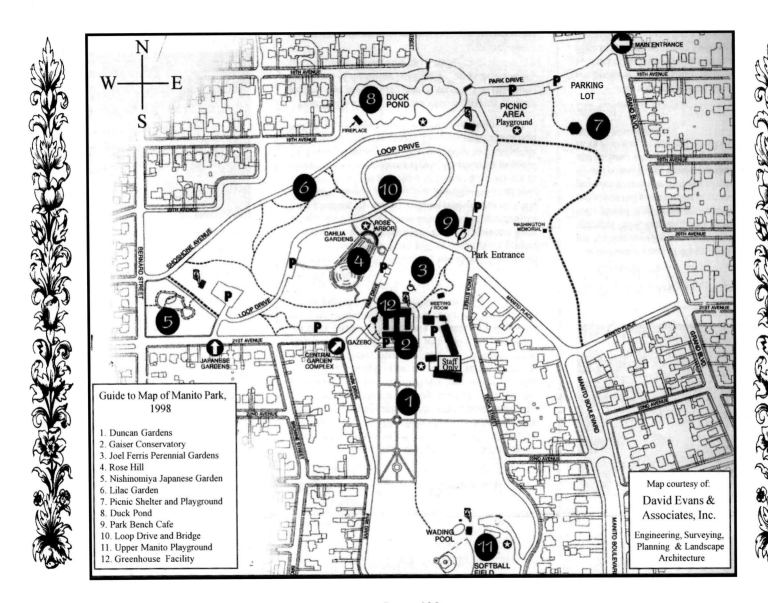

Guide to Map of Manito Park, 1998

1. Duncan Gardens
2. Gaiser Conservatory
3. Joel Ferris Perennial Gardens
4. Rose Hill
5. Nishinomiya Japanese Garden
6. Lilac Garden
7. Picnic Shelter and Playground
8. Duck Pond
9. Park Bench Cafe
10. Loop Drive and Bridge
11. Upper Manito Playground
12. Greenhouse Facility

Map courtesy of:

David Evans & Associates, Inc.

Engineering, Surveying, Planning & Landscape Architecture

A TOUR OF MANITO PARK AND THE BOTANICAL GARDENS TODAY

The numbers in the following information correspond with the map locations on page 120:

The Friends of Manito: Over the years Manito Park has received numerous awards for its beautiful gardens, which attract thousands of visitors every year. It is a popular location for people to gather for all sorts of events and a special place to honor loved ones with memorials. By the 1980s, time and budgetary constraints began to take their toll and the park started showing signs of deterioration. In response, John Dodson, then-horticultural supervisor of Manito Park, founded The Friends of Manito (TFM) in 1990.

Over the years, this nonprofit group, which presently has over 1000 members, has acted as a partner with the Parks Department, contributing substantial funding (in excess of $400,000 as of March 2004) towards improvements, preservation and promotion, as well as educational gardening activities and programs ("Sundays in the Garden" and the "Olmsted" series). Their annual plant sale became so popular, it is now held semiannually. Last year (2003), the sales grossed over $117,000, the net proceeds of which go directly into the park. Physical representations of this group's commitment to the park are evident throughout. An incomplete list of items for which they have provided funding include play equipment, benches, signage, sprinkler systems, greenhouse renovation, plant labels, pedestals, urns, new trees and other plants. This dedicated, hard-working group of volunteers have played an instrumental role in securing Manito's place as the gem of Spokane's park system. These contributions have earned them the Organizational Citation of Merit Award, an annual award given by the Washington Recreation and Park Association, Inc.

1. Duncan Garden: The formal European-style garden, directly south of the Gaiser Conservatory, was originally called the Sunken Garden. In February of 1941, the garden was officially renamed in honor of Park Superintendent John W. Duncan, who designed and began its development in 1912. During his tenure, the gardens contained many diversified plant species, including roses and perennials. A grape arbor was located at the far end in the rose garden. The garden's focal point is a large granite fountain, donated in 1956 in memory of Louis M. Davenport, a longtime park supporter and park board member, by Davenport's widow Verus and son Lewis.

Laurence R. Hamblen and Louis M. Davenport, both longtime park board members, in the Duncan Garden in August 1941. Hamblen also served as park board president and Davenport as vice-president. (Photo courtesy Spokane Parks & Recreation Dept.)

Over the years, the garden has undergone a number of revisions. In 1996, under the direction of Jim Flott, then-horticulture manager for Manito (and presently the urban forester for the Spokane Parks Department), and Debbie Goodwin, landscape architect, the most recent renovation was completed. At a cost of about $35,000, funded primarily through The Friends of Manito and Associated Garden Clubs of Spokane, the ratio of floral gardens to lawn was increased and a beautiful reflection pool was added at the south end. The new design won an award from the Washington Association of Landscape Professionals. TFM are presently moving ahead with plans for a gazebo – a centennial gift – to be situated south of the reflection pool. A vibrant array of colorful annuals, which now include displays of All American Annuals, make the Duncan Garden a popular site for summer chamber music concerts and weddings, and provides a scenic backdrop for photographers.

The Davenport Fountain, built in memory of L. M. Davenport in 1956, is the centerpiece of the Duncan Garden. The Gaiser Conservatory (background) was dedicated in 1988 in honor of Dr. David Gaiser. The inset photo, courtesy of Daniel and Jennifer Cox, was taken at their wedding reception in July 1990 in the Duncan Garden, a popular site for summer weddings. Daniel and Jennifer now (2004) have four daughters: Alexandra, Anna, Audrey and Amalina. (Bamonte photo, 1998)

2. Gaiser Conservatory and Greenhouses: The first greenhouses at Manito Park were moved from Liberty Park in 1904 and situated near the 20th Avenue entrance. New greenhouses were constructed at the current location in 1912, which were replaced in 1974. After many years of service, those are gradually being replaced by state-of-the-art greenhouses constructed of a triple-thick layer of polycarbonate, and equipped with fans, heaters and motorized thermal curtains that can be opened or closed to control the interior temperature. The first prototype was built in 2003 under the supervision of Steve Gustafson, horticulture supervisor since 2000. The costs for the initial phase of the greenhouse renovation, which also included thermal curtains in the Gaiser Conservatory and two new polyvinyl growing houses, was $330,000. An immediate return on investment is being realized in the cost savings to heat and cool the greenhouses and in providing more space for TFM and the Associated Garden Clubs to raise plants for the fund-raising sales.

The central dome of the conservatory was enlarged in 1988 and dedicated to the memory of Dr. David Gaiser, longtime park patron and former park board member appointed by Mayor Neal Fosseen. This popular attraction, which contains tropical, subtropical and

Robin Briley (right) and Jim Bolser (center), of Peak Video Productions, interviewing Michael D. Stone, director of the Spokane Parks and Recreation Department, in the Gaiser Conservatory in January 2004 for a documentary on Manito Park. (Bamonte photo)

temperate plant specimens from around the world, is open to the public, free of charge, year around. An attractive new display case in the Gaiser Conservatory, funded by TFM, houses memoriam plaques to honor memorial gifts to the park.

3. Ferris Perennial Garden: This garden, originally the site of an "old-fashioned" garden, was established by John Duncan around 1940 directly north of the office (headhouse) building (see right). It was named in honor of, Joel E. Ferris, a former park board member and popular civic leader following his death in 1960. This garden, which was renovated in 1996-1997 to enlarge the beds, contains over 300 plant species – all identified by markers. During the growing season, its ever-changing array of colors and textures offer

an informal counterpart to Duncan Garden's formal style. The centerpiece of the Butterfly Garden in the southeast corner of this garden is a memorial bird bath fountain donated by Mr. and Mrs. Alfred Hengen in memory of their daughter, Helen Hengen, a young Spangle aviatrix who lost her life in 1945 on her final flight test for her pilot's license.

Catherine "Cay" Betts (Williams), the second "Miss Spokane" – Spokane's official city hostess – and friends in the Ferris Perennial Garden, circa 1940. From left, Janet Campbell (Treyz), Cay, Connie Crommelin (Richardson), Janet Martin (Allan) and Pat Bartlett (Bulkley). (Photo courtesy Cay Williams)

4. Rose Hill: Situated on the hill west of the perennial garden, the formal beds contain about 1,500 rose bushes in over 150 varieties. Old-fashioned roses border sections of the garden, reminiscent of the profusion of roses growing wild at the time Francis Cook named it Montrose Park ("mountains of roses"). Manito Park is the

The Nishinomiya Japanese Garden was created as a tribute to the sister-city relationship with Nishinomiya, Japan. Nagao Sakurai, a former landscape architect for Tokyo's Imperial Palace, designed the garden. In 1998 the 24' arched ceremonial bridge, shown here, replaced three aging bridges. It was constructed of purpleheart, a durable tropical wood, on a steel frame. When it was installed, the wood was a brilliant purplish red, which gradually aged to grey. The $80,000 cost was jointly financed by the City, Spokane Parks and Recreation Dept., Friends of Manito and Associated Garden Clubs. (Bamonte photo 2004)

site of many memorials, especially in the rose garden. A pergola, 76 feet in diameter composed of 14 Tuscan columns for climbing roses, honors the late professional photographer Erna Bert Nelson, a generous benefactor to Spokane parks. It will be mirrored at the opposite end by a smaller pergola, with a 30-foot diameter and 16-foot radius, a centennial gift from TFM. The nearby sundial is a memorial to Mr. and Mrs. R. Jackson Wortman's two sons: Jacob J. Wortman, who died at age 15 after a lingering illness, and Ward K. Wortman, a Air Corps fighter pilot killed in action. Numerous rose bushes have also been donated as memorials.

John Duncan conceived the idea of the rose garden on Rose Hill and, before his retirement, planted some domestic roses along the hillside below. However, the cooperative project between the Spokane Parks and Recreation Department and the Spokane Rose Society did not materialize until Harold Abbott's tenure as park superintendent. In 1948 the Rose Society proposed a rose garden be established at Manito to serve as both a test garden and for memorial roses. Two years later, they donated $500 to launch the project. In 2003, for the thirteenth time, the showcase display earned Rose Hill the national All-American Rose Selections Award for Outstanding Maintenance, due in large part to the loving attention of gardener Steve Smith and his assistant, Tuong Nguyen.

5. Nishinomiya Japanese Garden:
In 1961 Mayor Neal Fosseen and his wife, Helen, initiated a Sister City program between Spokane and Nishinomiya, Japan. The concept of this Japanese garden emerged as a symbol of this relationship; Nishinomiya reciprocated by planting a lilac garden in Japan.

There is little wonder that the Japanese Garden is one of the most photographed areas of the park. The beauty of a Japanese garden is in its natural appearance, which, in fact, is methodically and meticulously designed with careful selection and placement of all the various elements. Nearly everything in the garden has symbolic significance – from the direction the water flows to the placement of the rocks – all designed to bring man into harmony with nature. The tranquil serenity and beauty inspires quiet contemplation.

This exquisite garden, in a corner of Manito Park bounded by Bernard and 21st, is sustained by the dedicated efforts of numerous individuals. The Japanese community's active involvement is led by Ed Tsutakawa, who chose the site and was instrumental in its early development. Nagao Sakurai, a former chief landscape architect for the Imperial Palace in Tokyo, designed the garden. Before its completion, Mr. Sakurai suffered a stroke, leaving him partially paralyzed. With the devoted assistance of Polly Mitchell Judd (then-president of Spokane Federation of Gardeners) and Ed Tsutakawa, Mr. Sakurai continued supervising with painstaking precision, from his wheelchair, until his deteriorating health forced his return to Japan. Shosuke Nagai, Hirohiko Kawai and Masakazu Tsushima are credited with bringing the project to completion. Following years of planning, fund-raising, construction and landscaping, the garden was dedicated by dignitaries from both cities during Expo '74. Over the years, some changes and improvements have taken place, the most recent of which include a new (1998) ceremonial bridge and, in 2004, a replacement fence surrounding the garden and a new handicap accessible entrance on Shoshone Avenue.

A familiar winter sight, circa 1941, at the ever-popular sledding hill, located adjacent to Grand Boulevard just east of the picnic grounds. In the early 1900s, another entrance to the park, located at 19th Avenue, was at the base of this hill.
(Wallace Gamble photo courtesy Spokane Parks and Recreation Department)

The scenic Loop Drive passes under and over this arched stone bridge, seen here in January 2004. (Bamonte photo)

6. Lilac Garden: The lilac garden was conceived in the fall of 1941 when the Spokane Garden Clubs presented 60 lilac bushes to the city. The garden, situated slightly southwest of the duck pond, contains many varieties of lilacs, Spokane's official flower. Buffalo roamed this area when the zoo was in existence. In 2003 the lilac garden was expanded to the west. The Boy Scouts built trails and planted 27 new lilac bushes, funded by the Lilac Society.

7. Picnic Shelter and Playground: In 1961 the Spokane Rotary Clubs donated a large picnic shelter near the 18th and Grand entrance. It contains fire pits, charcoal grills and picnic tables. In the early 1900s, a channel of water from the present pond extended through this area to Grand. At that time, there were entrances to the park from Grand at 19th and 20th, and a baseball field north of 19th. The popular sledding hill is east of the shelter, adjacent to Grand. In 1998 an attractive new playground, designed by Debbie Goodwin, landscape architect for the parks, was constructed west of the shelter.

8. Duck Pond: The pond began as a larger body of water called Mirror Lake. The spring-fed lake was always a popular site for year-around activities. A basalt rock fireplace, built near the west end of the pond in 1955, is a memorial to Lt. Lawrence Rist, an Air Force officer killed in action during the Korean War. (For more discussion on the present-day duck pond, please refer to page 113.)

9. Park Bench Cafe: Built in 1923, the "peanut shack" sold snacks for park visitors and peanuts for the monkeys. It is located at the intersections of Manito Place, Tekoa and Loop Drive, once the site of a natural pond (see pages 98-99). A private vendor sells refreshments during the summer months.

10. Loop Drive and Bridge: A scenic route through Manito Park is open in the summer months. The arched stone bridge, built in the 1930s, reflects the architectural design of the early park buildings.

Two bathing beauties and a Graham convertible at the Manito pond in 1937. (Libby Studio photo, MAC L87-1.12098-37)

11. Upper Manito Playground: Grading for the playground and softball field at the south end of the park in 1912 was in response to the 1907 Olmsted report's observation that the park did not have an adequate play field. Tennis courts and a lawn bowling green were also built in this area. A wading pool was added in 1920. Charles Balzer, the first park superintendent, built the first playground equipment in two separate locations at Manito. After the park board was formed, playground development became a priority. A new playground was installed in 2001.

12. Headhouse: Built in 1912, the basalt rock building directly north of the greenhouses serves as the administrative offices for the park horticulture staff and The Friends of Manito.

Manito Park has always been, and remains, Spokane's favorite park. It has the largest naturally wild, unspoiled tract of land within the city parks system. Preserving the natural character of this open space has not always been easy. Throughout its history, numerous proposals to establish commercial enterprises at Manito – including a Ferris wheel, merry-go-round, booths to sell souvenirs, and exhibits of all sorts – have been rejected. The park board's position has reflected the desires of its founders, such as Francis Cook and Aubrey White, to preserve beautiful open spaces for outdoor recreation and to enjoy nature. In the early 1990s, a movement to create a master plan for Manito included adding huge parking lots and a multipurpose meeting center in an undeveloped natural area. The City quickly experienced how deeply people felt about preserving *their* park's pristine beauty; the plan was rejected. A second plan, tailored to the public's input, is now being followed. The Parks Department faces an ongoing challenge of maintaining the beauty of the park while serving the changing needs and desires of a diversified public, all within budgetary constraints. Supporters are fiercely protective of Manito; many individuals (primarily through involvement in The Friends of Manito), garden clubs, service organizations and the Spokane Parks Foundation work with great dedication to preserve and enhance its natural beauty. The magnitude and magnificence of this park and a public dedicated to its preservation is one of Spokane's most priceless treasures.

Spokane County Pioneers' annual picnic, held on July 15, 1922 at Manito Park. *(Photo courtesy Cheney Museum)*

The Ferris Perennial Garden in the 1940s. *(Hand-painted photo courtesy Spokane Parks and Recreation Department)*

The majority of the color photographs in the following section are courtesy of photographers Carolyn Starner and Barbara Murray of Spokane and Bryan Trent of Graham, Washington. Please note captions for more information about these artists.

Looking south over the Ferris Perennial Garden and the headhouse, circa 2000. *(Photo courtesy The Friends of Manito)*

Butterfly Garden in the Ferris Perennial garden (left) and the rock garden below Rose Hill. *(Courtesy Carolyn Starner, photographer)*

Another perspective of the rock garden *(Courtesy Carolyn Starner, photographer)* ***and (right) a pathway through the Ferris Perennial Garden.*** *(Winning entry in 2002 The Friends of Manito photo contest courtesy Barbara Murray, photographer)*

The Erna Bert Nelson pergola in Manito Park's Rose Garden. *(Photo courtesy Barbara Murray. After retiring from her private practice as an optometric physician, Barbara turned her passion for gardening and photography into a business. Her photography has appeared in a number of regional publications.)*

Looking north toward the Gaiser Conservatory from the reflection pool in the Duncan Garden. *(Courtesy Carolyn Starner. Carolyn has blended her artistry as an interior designer and master gardener with her eye for photography in her upcoming (Spring 2004) book **Emerald Journey: A Walk Through Northwest Gardens**. She shot many of the photos used in this section for that book project.)*

Visitors to the Gaiser Conservatory are greeted by lush green and bright spots of color year around. (Bamonte photos, 2004)

The Duncan Garden in full bloom. This photo was taken from the bucket of a cherry-picker. *(Photo courtesy Barbara Murray, photographer)*

The Lilac Garden in Manito Park. *(Photo courtesy Carolyn Starner, photographer)*

The ceremonial bridge in the Nisinomiya Japanese Garden. *(Photo courtesy Carolyn Starner, photograper)*

The Nishinomiya Japanese Garden. *(Photo courtesy Carolyn Starner, photographer)*

The Nishinomiya Japanese Garden. *(Photo courtesy Carolyn Starner, photographer)*

A rose from Manito's rose garden and (right) the Nishinomiya Japanese Garden. (Photos courtesy photographer Bryan Trent, an avid outdoorsman who turned his photography hobby into a stock photography business called **Scenic Northwest Photography,** www.bryantrentphotography.com)

The Nishinomiya Japanese Garden and the Manito duck pond. (Photos courtesy Barbara Murray)

Selected Bibliography and Resources:

Bean, Margaret, *Age of Elegance*, 1968

Becher, Edmund T., *Spokane Corona, Era & Empires*, 1974

Board of Park Commissioners, Spokane, Annual reports

Durham, Nelson W., *Spokane and the Inland Empire, Volume I-Ill*, 1912

Dyar, Ralph, *News for an Empire*, 1952

Eastern Washington State Historical Society/MAC, Research Library Archives

Edwards, Rev. Jonathan, *An Illustrated History of Spokane County, Washington*, 1900

Fahey, John, *Shaping Spokane: Jay P. Graves and His Times*, 1994

Fuller, George W., *The Inland Empire*, Volume I-III, 1928

Hyslop, Robert B., *Spokane Building Blocks*, 1983

Jenson, Derrick and Draffin, George with John Osborn, MD, *Railroads and Clearcuts*

Kardong, Don and Schofield, Phil, *Bloomsday, A City in Motion*, 1989

King, E. W., *Coast Magazine*, November, 1907

Matthews, Henry C., *Kirtland Cutter, Architect in the Land of Promise*, 1998

McAlester, Virginia and Lee, *A Field Guide to American Houses, 1990*

McLean, Robert Craik, *The Western Architect*, Volume 12, Sept. 1908

Minnesota State Historical Society, Saint Paul, Archives (1888 to 1889)

Morning Review, The, selected articles

Municipal Code of the City of Spokane, The, 1892

Nolan, Edward W., *A Guide to the Cutter Collection, 1984*

Ogle, George A. & Co., *Standard Atlas of Spokane County*, 1912

Peltier, Jerome, *Northwest History, Articles from the Pacific N. W. Quarterly*, 1996

Pioneer Title Company, Archives (1886 to 1903)

Roberts, Ann, *Spokane County Cemetery Guide*, 1989

Robinson, C. W., *Spokane Falls and Its Exposition*, 1890

Spokan Times, The (both daily and weekly editions), selected articles

Spokan Times, The, (1879 to 1882)

Spokane County, State of Washington, Superior Court Case, Number 8425

Spokane County, Territorial Court Case Files, Numbers: 2264, 2493, 2017, 1459

Spokane County Title Company, Archives (1872 to 1926)

Spokane Daily Chronicle, selected articles

Spokane Daily Times, selected articles

Spokane Falls Review, The, selected articles

Spokane Parks and Recreation Department, *Spokane Park Board Minutes*

Spokane Public Library, Northwest Room, Archives

Spokane Weekly Chronicle and Review, The, selected articles

Spokane-Washington Improvement Company, *Brochure on Manito Park* , 1907

Spokesman Review, The, selected articles

Stricker, Clyde Thomas, *Purchasing a Mountain*

The Ballard Plannery Inc., Catalogue, Spokane, Washington, circa 1908

Washington State, Archives and Records Management Division

Washington State Archives, Eastern Region in Cheney, Manito Park Records

Western Historical Publishing Company, *History of North Washington*, 1904

Wright County (Minnesota) Historical Society, Archives (1888 to 1889)

Manito Park's main entrance, circa 1905.

Postcard photo courtesy Bill Stewart